AQA Religious Studies A
St Mark's Gospel

GCSE

Sheila Butler

Series editor

Cynthia Bartlett

OXFORD
UNIVERSITY PRESS

Great Clarendon Street, Oxford, OX2 6DP, United Kingdom

Oxford University Press is a department of the University of Oxford.
It furthers the University's objective of excellence in research, scholarship,
and education by publishing worldwide. Oxford is a registered trade mark of
Oxford University Press in the UK and in certain other countries

First published by Nelson Thornes Ltd in 2009
This edition published by Oxford University Press in 2014

British Library Cataloguing in Publication Data
Data available

978-1-4085-0458-1

6

Printed in India

Acknowledgements

Cover photograph: Rex Features / Jim Ryce
Page make-up: Pantek Arts Ltd, Maidstone

Text acknowledgements

Scripture quotations taken from the Holy Bible, New International Version.
Copyright © 1978, 1984 by International Bible Society. Used by permission of
Hodder & Stoughton, a division of Hodder Headline Ltd. All rights reserved.
'NIV' is a registered trademark of International Bible Society. UK trademark
number 1448790; Papias from *The Gospel of St Mark*, translated by W. Barclay,
St Andrew's Press 1957; Sheila Cassidy quote taken from *Made for Laughter*,
published and copyright 2006 by Darton Longman and Todd Ltd, London,
and used by permission of the publishers; *The Gospel according to St Mark* by M.
Hooker, published by Continuum Books 2001, reproduced by kind permission
of Continuum International Publishing Group; Sybil Phoenix, The 30 second
interview – see www2.lewisham.gov.uk/lbl/documents/news/lewishamlife/
jul07/30second.pdf; Maria Skobtzova (Mother Maria of Ravensbruck), from
her diary; Sister Helen Prejean's words reprinted by permission of Salt of
the Earth, copyright 1997 (http://salt.claretianpubs.org). Salt of the Earth is
published by the Claretians, 205 West Monroe, Chicago, IL 60606.

Photo acknowledgements

Alamy: 1.4A; 2.8A; 3.4C; 3.6B; 3.9A; 3.10B; 4.3B; 5.5A; 5.10B; 6.3A. **Art
Archive:** 2.6C; 3.1A; 3.5A; 4.8A. Corbis: 2.2B; 3.3C; 3.8B; 3.9B; 3.13A; 5.7B; 5.9B;
6.10B. **Fotolia:** 1.3B; 1.6C; 1.6D; 1.9B; 2.5D; 2.9A; 2.9C; 3.1C; 3.10C; 4.1A; 5.2B;
5.5B; 5.11B; 6.9A. **Getty Images:** 1.1C; 1.10B; 3.11A; CO5; 5.8B; 6.4C; 6.7C.
Graham Dunn: 5.2D. **iStockphoto:** CO1; 1.2A; 1.2B; 1.3C; 1.3E; 1.4B; 1.5A;
1.5B; 1.6A; 1.6B; 1.7A; 1.7B; 1.8A; 1.8B; 1.9A; 1.9C; 1.9D; 1.10A; CO2; 2.1B; 2.2A;
2.3B; 2.3C; 2.4A; 2.4b; 2.4C; 2.5A; 2.5B; 2.5C; 2.6B; 2.7A; 2.8B; 2.9B; CO3; 3.1B;
3.3A; 3.3B; 3.4A; 3.4B; 3.6C; 3.7A; 3.7B; 3.7C; 3.8A; 3.9C; 3.10A; 3.11A; 3.12A;
3.12B; CO4; 4.1B; 4.2A; 4.2B; 4.3A; 4.4A; 4.4B; 4.4C; 4.5A; 4.5B; 4.6A; 4.7A; 4.7B;
4.7C; 5.1A; 5.1B; 5.2A; 5.2C; 5.3A; 5.3B; 5.3C; 5.3D; 5.4A; 5.4B; 5.6B; 5.7A; 5.7C;
5.8A; 5.9A; 5.10A; 5.10C; 5.11A; CO6; 6.1A; 6.2A; 6.3B; 6.3C; 6.4A; 6.5A; 6.5B;
6.5C; 6.5D; 6.6A; 6.7A; 6.7B; 6.8A; 6.9B; 6.9C; 6.9D; 6.10A. **Mercy Ships UK:**
6.2B. **PA Photos:** 6.1B. **Peter Reed/SVP.org.uk:** 6.8B. **Photofusion:** 1.3D.
The Trustees of the British Museum: 3.6A. **Topfoto:** 3.2A; 3.8C; 5.6A.

Contents

Introduction   5

1 Background to Mark's Gospel   8

1.1   What is a gospel?   8

1.2   Authorship, date and location of Mark's Gospel   10

1.3   From Jerusalem to Rome   12

1.4   Sources behind Mark's Gospel (1)   14

1.5   Sources behind Mark's Gospel (2)   16

1.6   Reasons for writing the gospel (1)   18

1.7   Reasons for writing the gospel (2)   20

1.8   Opposition and persecution   22

1.9   Mark's Gospel as good news for 1st-century Christians   24

1.10   Mark's Gospel as good news for 21st-century Christians   26

Chapter 1 Assessment guidance   28

2 Jesus' ministry   30

2.1   Roman rule in Palestine   30

2.2   Religious and political groups in Palestine   32

2.3   Religious institutions   34

2.4   An overview of Jesus' ministry   36

2.5   Jesus' baptism   38

2.6   Jesus' temptation   40

2.7   Caesarea Philippi (1)   42

2.8   Caesarea Philippi (2)   44

2.9   The transfiguration   46

Chapter 2 Assessment guidance   48

3 Jesus' suffering, death and Resurrection   50

3.1   The entry into Jerusalem   50

3.2   The anointing and arrangements for betrayal   52

3.3   The Last Supper   54

3.4   Jesus in Gethsemane   56

3.5   Jesus' trial before the Sanhedrin   58

3.6   Jesus' trial before Pilate   60

3.7   The crucifixion and burial (1)   62

3.8   The crucifixion and burial (2)   64

3.9   The crucifixion and burial (3)   66

3.10   Jesus' Resurrection (1)   68

3.11   Jesus' Resurrection (2)   70

3.12   Jesus' Resurrection (3)   72

Chapter 3 Assessment guidance   74

4 The Person of Jesus   76

4.1   Jesus the teacher and miracle worker   76

4.2   The feeding of the five thousand (1)   78

4.3   The feeding of the five thousand (2)   80

4.4   Titles for Jesus: Christ/Messiah (1)   82

4.5   Titles for Jesus: Christ/Messiah (2)   84

4.6   Titles for Jesus: Son of Man (1)   86

4.7   Titles for Jesus: Son of Man (2)   88

4.8   Titles for Jesus: Son of God   90

Chapter 4 Assessment guidance   92

5 **Jesus' relationship with others 94**

5.1	The Sabbath in the time of Jesus	94
5.2	Jesus and the Jewish authorities: the Sabbath	96
5.3	Jesus and the Jewish authorities: the Temple Court	98
5.4	Jesus and the Jewish authorities: paying Roman taxes	100
5.5	Christian attitudes to authority	102
5.6	Jesus and the outcast (1)	104
5.7	Jesus and the outcast (2)	106
5.8	Jesus and the outcast (3)	108
5.9	Jesus and the sick (1)	110
5.10	Jesus and the sick (2)	112
5.11	Jesus and the sick (3)	114

Chapter 5 Assessment guidance 116

6 **Discipleship** **118**

6.1	The Twelve: the calling of the first four disciples	118
6.2	The Twelve: the mission	120
6.3	The Twelve: Peter	122
6.4	The Twelve: role models	124
6.5	The Kingdom of God: parables	126
6.6	The Kingdom of God: the cost of discipleship	128
6.7	The Kingdom of God: the rich man and wealth	130
6.8	The Kingdom of God: service	132
6.9	The Kingdom of God: the greatest commandments	134
6.10	The Kingdom of God: the widow at the treasury	136

Chapter 6 Assessment guidance 138

Glossary 140

Index 142

The publisher has worked hard to ensure that this book offers you support for your GCSE course.

■ How to use this book

Learning Objectives

At the beginning of each section or topic you'll find a list of Learning Objectives based on the requirements of the specification, so you can make sure you are covering key points for this course.

Objectives

Objectives

Objectives

Objectives

First objective.

Second objective.

Study Tips

Don't forget to look at the Study Tips throughout the book to help you with your study and prepare for your exam.

> **Study tip**
>
> Don't forget to look at the Study Tips throughout the book to help you with your study and prepare for your exam.

Practice Questions

These offer opportunities to practise questions in the style that you may encounter in your exam so that you can be fully prepared on the day.

Practice questions are reproduced by permission of the Assessment and Qualifications Alliance.

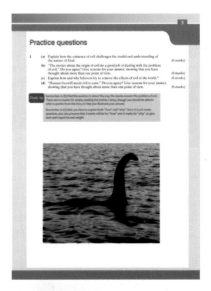

GCSE St Mark's Gospel

This book is written specifically for GCSE students studying the AQA Religious Studies Specification A, Unit 5: *St Mark's Gospel*. It covers Mark's account of Jesus' life and teaching in Palestine, the background to his ministry, and Mark's insight into the significance of Jesus for Christians.

Remember, use only material from Mark's Gospel in the examination. Make sure you know and understand the set Bible passages – included where possible, otherwise referenced in a Link box in the form 'Mark 1:1' to indicate Mark Chapter 1 verse 1. You must also understand all Key Terms: look for the Key Terms boxes or use the Links boxes/Glossary to locate the explanations.

■ Topics in this unit

In the examination you will be asked to answer questions taken from any of the topics. Topics may be mixed within questions. Chapters in this book are arranged to cover the following topics:

Background to Mark's Gospel

This topic examines what led to Mark writing his gospel and its nature and purpose for Christians in the 1st and 21st centuries.

Jesus' ministry

This topic examines key 'watershed' events in the ministry of Jesus and their significance for Jesus, his disciples and Christians.

Jesus' suffering, death and resurrection

This topic examines Jesus' passion, death and resurrection and their significance for Jesus, for those involved at the time and for Christians.

The Person of Jesus

This topic considers Mark's portrayal of Jesus as teacher and miracle worker, as Christ/Messiah, Son of Man and Son of God, and the significance of his portrayal of Jesus for Christians.

Jesus' relationships with others

This topic examines Jesus' encounters with Jewish authorities, the outcast and the sick, and the significance of these relationships for Christian attitudes in the 21st century.

Discipleship

This topic studies stories and teachings relating to the Twelve, especially Peter, and the nature of the kingdom of God and the demands of discipleship, together with their significance for 21st century Christians.

■ Assessment guidance

Questions testing your knowledge and understanding will range from short answer questions to more extended questions, carrying from one to six marks each. Evaluation questions, testing your ability to give your opinion and/or argue differing viewpoints, carry either three or six marks. Practice questions are given in the assessment guidance sections, one at the end of each chapter. Each assessment section also has a sample answer for you to mark. Use the mark schemes below to guide you.

Examination questions will test two assessment objectives:

AO1	Describe, explain and analyse, using knowledge and understanding.	50%
AO2	Use evidence and reasoned argument to express and evaluate personal responses, informed insights and differing viewpoints.	50%

Levels of response mark schemes

The quality of your written communication will also be taken into account – how clearly you express yourself and how well you communicate your meaning.

The grid below also gives you some guidance on the sort of quality expected at different levels.

Levels	Criteria for AO1	Criteria for AO2	Quality of written communication	Marks
0	Nothing relevant or worthy of credit	An unsupported opinion or no relevant evaluation	The candidate's presentation, spelling, punctuation and grammar seriously obstruct understanding	0 marks
Level 1	Something relevant or worthy of credit	An opinion supported by simple reason	The candidate presents some relevant information in a simple form. The text produced is usually legible. Spelling, punctuation and grammar allow meaning to be derived, although errors are sometimes obstructive	1 mark
Level 2	Elementary knowledge and understanding, e.g. two simple points	An opinion supported by one developed reason or two simple reasons		2 marks
Level 3	Sound knowledge and understanding	An opinion supported by one well developed reason or several simple reasons. **N.B. Candidates who make no religious comment should not achieve more than Level 3**	The candidate presents relevant information in a way which assists with the communication of meaning. The text produced is legible. Spelling, punctuation and grammar are sufficiently accurate not to obscure meaning	3 marks
Level 4	A clear knowledge and understanding with some development	An opinion supported by two developed reasons with reference to religion		4 marks
Level 5	A detailed answer with some analysis, as appropriate	Evidence of reasoned consideration of two different points of view, showing informed insights and knowledge and understanding of religion	The candidate presents relevant information coherently, employing structure and style to render meaning clear. The text produced is legible. Spelling, punctuation and grammar are sufficiently accurate to render meaning clear	5 marks
Level 6	A full and coherent answer showing good analysis, as appropriate	A well-argued response, with evidence of reasoned consideration of two different points of view showing informed insights and ability to apply knowledge and understanding of religion effectively		6 marks

Note: In evaluation answers to questions worth only 3 marks, the first three levels apply. Questions which are marked out of 3 marks do not ask for two views, but reasons for your own opinion.

Successful study of this unit will result in a Short Course GCSE award. Study of one further unit will provide a Full Course GCSE award. Other units in Specification A which may be taken to achieve a Full Course GCSE award are:

- Unit 1: Christianity
- Unit 2: Christianity: Ethics
- Unit 3: Roman Catholicism
- Unit 4: Roman Catholicism: Ethics
- Unit 7: Philosophy of Religion
- Unit 8: Islam
- Unit 9: Islam: Ethics
- Unit 10: Judaism
- Unit 11: Judaism: Ethics
- Unit 12: Buddhism
- Unit 13: Hinduism
- Unit 14: Sikhism

N.B. Units 5 and 6 are a prohibited combination, so for a Full Course qualification you may **not** study both St Mark's Gospel (Unit 5) and St Luke's Gospel (Unit 6).

Θεοφανία...
...ίλιας δὲ ἐ Ἄἴνοσε το...
...σιας δὲ ἐ Ἄἴνοσε τον...
...ναι τον μαναοσῆ...
...Θίνοσε τον ἰωσίαν.
...ίαν και ἐν ἀδελφ...
...σρονίας

1 Background to Mark's Gospel

1.1 What is a gospel?

The New Testament

The New Testament forms the second part of the Christian Bible. It consists of 27 books written during the first two centuries of the Common Era (CE). The books fall into four main types:

- **gospels**
- history of the Early Church
- letters
- revelation (prophecy).

Their style, outlook, themes and purposes differ, but all were written for the early Christian churches that were developing across the Roman Empire, and all were written in Greek.

It took more than two centuries to decide which Christian writings should form the New Testament. The Church's leaders claimed that the authors whose writings were included were specially inspired by God. Some of those writings that were not included in the New Testament continued to be used by local churches. Others, such as the Gospel of Thomas, were denounced as containing heresy, or false beliefs.

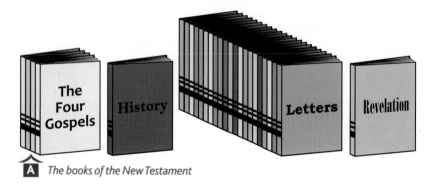

A The books of the New Testament

The special authority of the gospels

Because they contain the teaching of Jesus and stories about him, Christians have treasured the gospels. Most still believe that they contain the word of God and have a special **authority**, as their authors were guided by God. Some Christians believe that the inspiration came directly from God, and so the gospels have no mistakes. The stories about Jesus are, therefore, historically accurate, and Christians should obey all the teachings. However, other Christians believe that God may have inspired or guided the authors, but he did not prevent them from making mistakes or prevent changes from occurring as the stories were handed down. For these Christians, the *meaning* behind the stories is what really matters.

B Two views on the authority of the gospels

What is a gospel?

At first reading, people tend to assume that a gospel is either a piece of historical writing or a biography. But the word gospel means 'good news', and gospels have a particular purpose.

The nature of Mark's Gospel (Mark 1:1)

All the gospels are good news, written by a believer for other believers or for potential converts. The opening verse of Mark's Gospel makes this clear. It is not intended simply as an objectively written life of a 1st-century Palestinian Jew called Jesus. Mark's Gospel is written from faith and for faith. Its author was a Christian writing for a particular Christian community. By proclaiming the good news about Jesus, Mark's Gospel aimed to strengthen and deepen faith and commitment.

C   *Preaching the good news today*

Beliefs and teachings

The beginning of the gospel about Jesus Christ, the Son of God.

Mark 1:1

Activity

1 a In small groups, make lists of features that you would expect to be in a piece of historical writing (e.g. dates of events) and in a biography (e.g. date and place of birth).

   b Then read Mark 1–2 and 14–15. Note the ways in which these passages from Mark contain the features you have listed. Then note the ways in which they do not.

   c Finally, discuss the extent to which these passages could be called historical and/or biographical writings.

⌾links

For more information on how Mark's Gospel was, and still is, seen as good news to Christians, read pages 24–27.

Summary

You should now understand that the New Testament consists of writings many Christians believe to have been inspired by God; the term 'gospel' means 'good news'; and Mark's Gospel aims to tell the good news about Jesus to deepen faith.

Study tip

Ensure that you learn the meaning of the word 'gospel' as you might be asked for its definition in the exam.

Authorship, date and location of Mark's Gospel

■ Who wrote Mark's Gospel?

The evidence for Mark as author

Beliefs and teachings

Mark, who was Peter's interpreter, wrote down accurately, though not in order, all that he recollected of what Christ had said or done. For he was not a hearer of the Lord or a follower of his. He followed Peter, as I have said, at a later date, and Peter adapted his instruction to practical needs, without any attempt to give the Lord's words systematically. So that Mark was not wrong in writing down some things in this way from memory, for his one concern was neither to omit nor to falsify anything that he had heard.

Papias, an early Christian writer

Objectives

Know the traditional view of the authorship, date and location of Mark's Gospel.

Understand why there can be no certainty about this.

Consider whether this affects the credibility of Mark's Gospel.

Discussion activity

1 What words or phrases used by Papias suggest that Mark's Gospel is or is not a reliable account of the life and teaching of Jesus?

A man named Mark (sometimes known as John Mark) is referred to in the New Testament and in early Church tradition. It is claimed that he came from Jerusalem, and his mother, Mary, owned the house where Jesus held the Last Supper. Mark would not have been there himself (an eyewitness) for most of Jesus' ministry, but he might well have been in the house during that meal. The upper room where the Last Supper was held became the meeting point for Christians after Jesus' death, so Mark would have had contacts with the early Christian community. This supports the view that he was the author of the gospel.

There is a story, only in Mark's Gospel, about a mysterious man in Gethsemane who witnessed the arrest of Jesus and then ran off naked when the Temple guard tried to seize him. Some think that Mark was the young man – explaining why only he included this incident. Mark is also mentioned in the Acts of the Apostles, accompanying Barnabas and Paul to Cyprus. Other references to him in the New Testament suggest that in the 60s CE he was in Rome with Peter and Paul, and so he could have written the gospel. Finally, the Greek in Mark's Gospel is, at times, very clumsy: John Mark's first language was Aramaic, the language spoken widely in Palestine at that time, so it is likely that his Greek would not have been perfect.

Beliefs and teachings

A young man, wearing nothing but a linen garment, was following Jesus. When they seized him, he fled naked, leaving his garment behind.

Mark 14:51

∞ links

For the Last Supper and Jesus' arrest, see pages 54–57; for the young man in Gethsemane, see pages 14–15 and Mark 14:51–52.

A *Gethsemane*

When and where was the gospel written?

The date for the writing of this gospel cannot be fixed precisely. However, because of the contents of Mark 13, almost all New Testament scholars agree that Mark's Gospel was written around the time of the destruction of Jerusalem in 70 CE. Most scholars also think that Mark's Gospel was the first of the four New Testament gospels and that the other three used it as a source. Some who reject the traditional view of authorship think that Mark's Gospel might have been written in Syria or in Egypt, but the traditional view is that it was written in Rome.

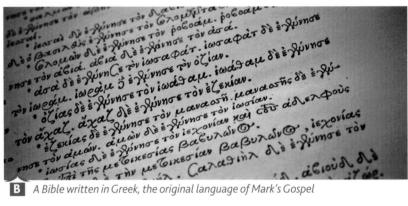

B   *A Bible written in Greek, the original language of Mark's Gospel*

Conclusion

There can be no certainty that the Mark of the New Testament was the author of Mark's Gospel. The traditional view, however, has him as author, writing in Rome around 70 CE, and this is the position taken in this book.

Discussion activity

2   We cannot be certain about where, when and by whom the gospel was written. Does this matter in assessing its reliability and its claim to give the good news about God and Jesus?

Activity

Using the information in these two pages, create a fact file on Mark. You could use these headings:

- 'The Last Supper'
- 'The arrest in Gethsemane'
- 'Barnabas and Paul' (also known as Saul)
- 'Mark in Rome'
- 'Papias'.

Use the following references to help you: Mark 14:51–52; Acts 12:25 and 13:4; Colossians 4:10.

Study tip

You do not need to know in detail all the information given here about Mark. But you should use it to be aware of his possible sources and to assess their reliability.

Extension activity

1   a   Look up the following New Testament passages:
- Acts 12:25–13:13; 15:36–39
- 2 Timothy 4:11
- Philemon 23–24
- 1 Peter 6:13 (NB: Rome was often referred to as Babylon in early Christian writings and 'son' is used here metaphorically).

   b   Use the information in these texts to extend your fact file on Mark.

Summary

You should now understand the traditional view about Mark's Gospel – that it was written in Rome shortly before or after 70 CE by John Mark – but you should also appreciate that there can be no absolute certainty about this.

1.3 From Jerusalem to Rome

■ The early Church

According to Acts of the Apostles, the centre of Christianity was in Jerusalem. The presence of Jesus' disciples gave the Church in Jerusalem a unique status. At first the Church consisted of Jews who believed that Jesus was the Messiah (see Links). They believed he had been wrongly killed, but had conquered death to be a living presence in their lives. Gradually, Gentiles (non-Jews) were attracted to the Christian faith and it became increasingly distinct from Judaism.

How Christianity spread

Many traders and pilgrims who visited Jerusalem were converted to Christianity during their stay. They took their new faith home with them, and so Christian communities sprang up in many other places. Paul and Barnabas became leaders of the Christian community at Antioch in Syria, and embarked from there on their first missionary journey, taking John Mark with them. By the middle of the 1st century, Christian communities were to be found in Asia Minor (modern Turkey), Greece, North Africa and Italy. There had been a Christian community in Rome long before Paul arrived there.

■ Rome in the 1st century

Rome, the centre of the Roman Empire, was in many ways like large cities in the modern Western world. Its population was very mixed racially and culturally, and its inhabitants practised a variety of religions. Many people, dissatisfied with established religions, were searching for something to satisfy them spiritually, provide clear moral guidance and make sense of their lives. Although few became full converts, many were attracted to Judaism because of its belief in one God and its high moral standards. They attended worship in the synagogue and were known as 'godfearers'. Others joined one of the many mystery religions that were popular at that time. These were cults with secret rites, and their members often shared sacred meals.

Rome attracted people from across the Empire who were hiding from the authorities, such as criminals and runaway slaves. They formed a social underclass, seen by the upper classes as a threat to the city's security and stability.

Objectives

Know how Christianity spread from its beginnings in Jerusalem.

Understand similarities between 1st-century Rome and modern cities, and how the backgrounds of early Christians, and Christianity's appeal to the disadvantaged, applied to 1st-century Rome.

∞ links

For an explanation of the term 'Messiah', see pages 82–85.

A *The 1st-century Roman Empire in the Mediterranean*

Research activity 🔍

The Mithras cult

1   a   Find out about this mystery religion. There are plenty of websites containing information.

    b   What similarities can you see between the Mithras cult and Christianity? Consider the early lives of Mithras and Jesus, the use of rites and sacred meals to form a sense of community, and their appeal to those without power and wealth.

■ The early Church in Rome

In the earliest days of the Church, most Christians were converts from Judaism. By the time Mark came to write his gospel around 70 CE, this was no longer the case, because Christianity appealed especially to the godfearers, and they offered their homes as places where Christians could meet. In many churches, Gentile Christians far outnumbered Jewish Christians. Christianity attracted converts from all classes of society. However, it held a special appeal for those who were overlooked, despised or exploited by those in power, especially women and slaves. This was because of teaching that racial, gender and social distinctions meant nothing to God. This was especially true of the Church in Rome, a city where people of many races, cultures and classes lived closely together.

Beliefs and teachings

You are all sons of God through faith in Christ Jesus, for all of you who were baptised into Christ have clothed yourselves with Christ. There is neither Jew nor Greek, slave nor free, male nor female, for you are all one in Christ Jesus.

Galatians 3:26–28

Activities

1 Find out about what life was like for slaves in the time of the Roman Empire. You might watch some of the film *Spartacus* or look at one of the websites listed in the Links opposite.

2 Imagine you are a slave in one of the Roman provinces, running away from your master and making your way to Rome, where you make contact with a group of Christians. Create a comic strip, telling your story from the time before your escape to your arrival in Rome and your decision to become a Christian.

∞ links

Websites giving information on slavery in ancient Rome:

www.pbs.org

www.bbc.co.uk

www.historyforkids.org

Discussion activity

1 a Mark's Gospel appealed to the lowest classes of society in the Roman world. Which groups would you see as the most marginalised in the modern world? The photos might give you some ideas to get started.

b Create a list in a small group and then share your ideas with another group, noting down any of their suggestions that you did not think of.

c Finally, as a whole-class activity, consider ways in which the dispossessed of today's world are similar to those of 1st-century Rome.

A Homeless man

B Drug addict

C Young slave worker

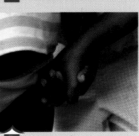

D AIDS orphans

Study tip

Remember the very mixed nature of the Church in Rome and Christianity's appeal to slaves and other powerless groups throughout your study of Mark's Gospel. This will help you to a deeper understanding of the gospel.

Summary

You should now know how the Church expanded from a small Jewish Christian community in Jerusalem to mainly Gentile Churches throughout the Mediterranean. You should understand that the Church in Rome was attractive to women, slaves and other disadvantaged groups.

■ Possible sources of information

The traditional theory is that Mark's Gospel was written in Rome in the late 60s CE by the Mark referred to in the New Testament. Assuming this is the case, Mark would have had access to many different sources and types of information on which to base his gospel.

Primary sources of information

The reliability of any information is generally increased if it comes from someone who was actually there – a primary **source**. Mark was not with Jesus during his **ministry**, but might have had access to those who were.

Peter

Papias states that Mark got much of the information for his gospel from Peter, one of Jesus' closest **disciples**. If true, this would account for the details in many of the stories. For instance, in his account of the calming of the storm, Mark said that Jesus was asleep on a pillow in the stern of the boat. Only Mark has this detail. The story of Jairus' daughter is very vivid. Even more importantly, Jesus' words are recorded in Aramaic rather than the usual Greek. Were the actual words that Jesus spoke remembered by Peter and then passed on to Mark?

∞ links

For an overview of Jesus' ministry, see Chapter 2; for more on discipleship, see Chapter 6.

For an overview of Jesus' ministry, see Chapter 2; for more on discipleship, see Chapter 6.

Objectives

Understand what primary sources of information Mark might have used when writing his gospel.

Key terms

Source: a text, statement, person, etc. that supplies information.

Ministry: this word means 'service'. When used with reference to Jesus, it refers to his three years' work of teaching and healing. His ministry began with his baptism and ended with his crucifixion.

Disciples: followers of Jesus; this term is often used to refer the first twelve followers of Jesus; any Christian, in any age, who lives their life according to Gospel values.

Activity

Read the story of Jairus' daughter in the Beliefs and teachings box. Make a note of those details which suggest that Mark might have heard the story from Peter, who was there.

Beliefs and teachings

He did not let anyone follow him except Peter, James and John the brother of James. When he came to the home of the synagogue ruler, Jesus saw a commotion. After he put them all out, he took the child's father and mother and the disciples who were with him, and went in where the child was. He took her by the hand and said to her, 'Talitha koum!' (which means, 'Little girl, I say to you, get up!'). Immediately the girl stood up and walked around (she was twelve years old). At this they were completely astonished. He gave strict orders not to let anyone know about this, and told them to give her something to eat.

Mark 5:37–38, 40–43

A *The healing of Jairus' daughter*

The twelve disciples

Mark would have known the other disciples of Jesus, as they met in his mother's house. Here he would have heard their stories of their time with Jesus.

Other eyewitnesses

Mark would probably have met others who had known Jesus, whose lives had sometimes been dramatically changed by the experience. For instance, after his cure, Bartimaeus went to Jerusalem for the Passover celebration, where Mark might have met him. Mark might also have learned details of the crucifixion from Simon of Cyrene, the man who carried Jesus' cross and whose sons were Christians in Rome. Or he might have heard them from the women who stood at a distance, who were part of the Christian community meeting in his mother's house.

Beliefs and teachings

A certain man from Cyrene, Simon, the father of Alexander and Rufus, was passing by on his way in from the country, and they forced him to carry the cross.

Mark 15:21

B *Simon of Cyrene helped carry the cross*

Personal experience

After the Last Supper, late at night, Mark might have seen the Temple guards being led by Judas, as their route to Gethsemane is thought to have passed his home. Sensing that Jesus was in danger, or simply wanting to know what was going on, he might then have followed them. He may have witnessed the arrest, before running from the guard.

Divine inspiration

Some Christians believe that Mark was directly inspired by God. The Jesus in the gospel would therefore not have been Mark's own 'take' on him. Rather, Mark would have represented Jesus according to God's guidance. These Christians believe that God directed Mark to include the stories and teachings in the gospel, that all Mark's sources would have been reliable and that everything in the gospel is correct. Others believe that Mark, as a human, was open to making mistakes and to interpreting what he heard.

∞links

Read more: the calming of the storm, pages 24–25; Jesus' final week, pages 54–67; Jairus' daughter and Bartimaeus, pages 112–115.

Summary

You should now know that Mark's primary sources for his gospel might include both people who were there and his own personal experience.

Study tip

Make sure that you know Mark's possible sources for his gospel. You might be asked to name some. You would gain marks for using the Beliefs and teachings box on page 14 to support Peter as a primary source.

■ Information flow in Roman times

A great deal of literature was produced in the early centuries of the Common Era, but books were handwritten, scarce and expensive. Most people were not literate and relied on oral tradition – the passing on of information by word of mouth. Mark would have received information from secondary sources – people who did not witness the events themselves – and it is likely that these sources were both written and oral.

■ Mark's written sources

These would have taken various forms: some almost like a short list, others more lengthy collections of writings.

Collections of teaching

Certain people were recognised in each Christian community as called by God to be teachers and preachers. Some of the stories about Jesus and his teachings were probably written down for their use. The construction of Mark's Gospel might give evidence of this. In Chapters 2 and 3 there is a collection of stories relating disagreements between Jesus and the religious authorities. In Chapter 4 several parables are grouped together.

The Passion narrative

From the earliest days, the events leading up to Jesus' crucifixion would have been told during the Eucharist and at the annual commemoration of his death. Many scholars think that **The Passion** story would have been written down early in the Church's existence, because it was so important.

∞ links

Read more: Jesus' disagreements with the authorities, Chapter 5; the parables, Chapter 6; the Eucharist, pages 54–55; and the Passion, pages 52–67.

Other written sources

Ur Markus

A few scholars speculate that Mark worked from an earlier gospel written in Aramaic (the spoken language in the time of Jesus). This is known as *Ur Markus*, a primitive version of Mark's Gospel, and might have been written earlier by Mark or by an unknown Christian.

Matthew's Gospel

Others claim that Matthew's Gospel was written before Mark's, and that Mark used it as the basis for his writing. (This is part of the 'synoptic problem', which looks at connections between the first three gospels.) The view of most, however, is that Mark's Gospel came first, and was the basis for the gospels of both Matthew and Luke.

> **Objectives**
>
> Understand what secondary sources of information Mark might have used when writing his gospel.
>
> Understand and assess views on the authority of Mark's Gospel.

> **Key terms**
>
> The Passion: the term used to describe Jesus' suffering prior to this death.

A *The Passion narrative has inspired artists for centuries*

Mark's oral sources

Much of Mark's information probably came from oral tradition, the most common way of passing on information at this time.

Paul and Barnabas

As they did not know Jesus personally, Paul and Barnabas would have been taught about his life and teachings. When Mark accompanied them to Cyprus, he would then have heard them passing on this teaching in their preaching.

How reliable were Mark's sources?

Reliable sources add to a book's authority, but opinions about Mark's sources differ. With oral tradition there is the possibility of exaggeration and change. Eyewitnesses might not remember accurately what happened decades earlier. The teaching in written sources might have been adapted to meet the needs of particular Christian communities.

Many Christians argue that those in the ancient world were accustomed to remembering and passing on information accurately, and used particular styles to make their words memorable. These Christians also claim that the disciples' experiences were so life-changing that they were unlikely to have forgotten any of it in the 35 years or so between the crucifixion and the writing of Mark's Gospel.

Many Christians also accept that there was some adaptation of material, but that Christian teachers would not have made major changes to teaching and then claim it came straight from Jesus. In his letters, for example, Paul distinguished carefully between the teachings that came from Jesus and the guidance of the Church. You can see this distinction in his guidance on marriage to the Christian community at Corinth.

B   *Paul's preaching often brought him trouble*

> **Beliefs and teachings**
>
> To the married I give this command (not I, but the Lord): A wife must not separate from her husband ... To the rest I say this (I, not the Lord): If any brother has a wife who is not a believer ...
>
> *1 Corinthians 7:10 and 12*

Summary

You should now understand that Mark might have used a variety of written and oral sources and that Christians hold differing views on the reliability of his sources and, therefore, on the authority of his gospel.

Discussion activities 👥

1. Work in groups of five. Two of the group should plan and then act out a short sketch in which they meet up in a café, discuss what they are going to eat and drink, order it from a waiter and then talk about a night out with a third friend. In the sketch, there should be a number of clear details or memorable phrases. One of the other three students should take notes. The non-actors should then try to pass on to another group the key details of the sketch. Discuss any differences in accuracy of recall between those who took notes and those relying on memory alone.

2. In a whole-class discussion, relate this activity to the issue of Mark's oral sources and their reliability. Remember that people in the ancient worlds were practised in the oral tradition. How might that affect people's memories? Were stories that were passed down orally more likely to be accurate in the ancient world than today?

1.6 Reasons for writing the gospel (1)

■ Themes in Mark's Gospel

Like all writers, Mark must have had particular points he wanted to get across to his readers, but he did not state them explicitly. By careful reading of his gospel, New Testament scholars have pointed to a number of themes that run through it. These could be the points Mark wanted to make, and might be among the reasons he wrote his gospel.

The identity of Jesus

Nowhere is Jesus' humanity more clearly presented than in Mark's Gospel. Mark shows us that Jesus was on occasion angry, or afraid of death; that he needed the support of his disciples; and that he thought God had deserted him. Yet, Mark also gives the impression of Jesus' great authority: in his teaching and healing; in controlling the forces of nature; and ultimately in overcoming death. Many Christians think that Mark's presentation of Jesus was intended to support Christians in Rome at a time of crisis. When they were afraid, or angry, they would feel that Jesus understood. Yet his authority and the triumph of his resurrection would have assured them that they could trust in him.

Many different titles are used for Jesus, and they also point to his identity. Central to this gospel is the theme of the 'Messianic Secret': Jesus did not want his true identity known.

> **Objectives**
>
> Understand the major themes running through Mark's Gospel.
>
> Understand their importance for Mark's readers.

⬤⬤ links

Read more about the Messianic Secret in Chapters 2 and 4.

Beliefs and teachings

Whenever the evil spirits saw him, they fell down before him and cried out, 'You are the Son of God.' But he gave them strict orders not to tell who he was.

Mark 3:11–12

Peter answered, 'You are the Christ.' Jesus warned them not to tell anyone about him.

Mark 8:29–30

As they were coming down the mountain, Jesus gave them strict orders not to tell anyone what they had seen until the Son of Man had risen from the dead.

Mark 9:9

Activity

1. a Read the following two groups of passages:

   Group 1   Group 2

   Mark 3:5; 11:15; 14:33–36; 15:34.   Mark 4:41; 9:2–3; 11:7–10; 15:39.

   b Write one sentence on each group of passages, showing how Jesus is portrayed in them.

   c Now read this statement: 'People can relate more easily to Jesus as a vulnerable man than as a being of great power and authority.' Using your reading of the two groups of passages, decide whether you agree with the statement or not. Explain your opinion.

A *Who was the Jesus of Mark's Gospel, a vulnerable man or a being of great power?*

Jesus' death and resurrection

In one of his letters, Paul pointed out that the idea of a crucified Messiah was offensive to Jews (who believed Old Testament teaching that it was a cursed death) and foolish to Gentiles (who were used to seeing criminals executed on crosses). Mark's Gospel needed to tackle this. Mark stresses the central importance of Jesus' death: from very early in his gospel he stated that Jesus' radical views would lead to his death. Throughout the second part of the gospel, Jesus repeatedly states that his imminent rejection, suffering and death are part of God's purpose. The gospel also shows that death was not the end. There are many references to Jesus' resurrection, and the gospel ends with his empty tomb. Christians were therefore meant to see the crucifixion in the light of the resurrection.

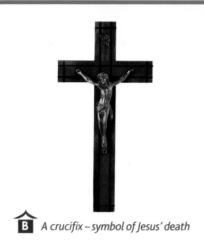

B *A crucifix – symbol of Jesus' death*

Discipleship and the Kingdom of God

A striking feature of Mark's Gospel is the way he describes the disciples repeatedly failing Jesus. Sometimes they lacked faith, or challenged his teachings, and finally they all abandoned him to his fate. One of them even betrayed him and another denied all knowledge of him. Yet, apart from the traitor, these were the men who became the leaders of the Early Church. Alongside this is Jesus' teaching on the demands of discipleship, including an incident where one rich man could not accept what Jesus asked of him, which was to give everything to the poor. Mark's Gospel also contains parables and other teaching on the Kingdom of God. Mark's readers knew from their own experience how difficult discipleship could be. The stories relating to the Twelve would have helped them and shown that even if their faith failed them at times, they could be forgiven. For instance, Peter denied Jesus, yet the young man at the empty tomb gave Peter a message that would change history.

C *A cross – symbol of Jesus' resurrection*

Activity

2 a Working in pairs, create a chart with four columns. Head the first column with the words 'Gospel reference' and the other columns with the three themes in Mark's Gospel: 'The identity of Jesus', 'Jesus' death and resurrection' and 'Discipleship and the Kingdom of God'. Write the following references down the first column: Mark 2:12; 3:6; 4:40; 8:31; 14:37; 15:34.

   b Read each reference and give a one sentence summary in the appropriate theme column.

   c Discuss how these passages might have strengthened the faith of early Christians.

∞ links

Read about the Passion predictions, Chapter 2; betrayal, death and resurrection, Chapter 3; denials, discipleship and the Kingdom of God, Chapter 6; and parables, Chapter 6.

Summary

You should now know and understand the significance of the three important themes in Mark's Gospel: the identity of Jesus; the significance of Jesus' death and resurrection; and the nature of discipleship. All these related directly to the experience of the early Christians in Rome.

Study tip

Understanding how the key themes relate to the circumstances of the 1st century Church in Rome will help you appreciate better the reasons for Mark writing his gospel.

*tò iweqéu. iwe...
oúias dè ex Wúnnoe tòv...
àvat dè ex Wúnnoe toúv...
...ooe tòv maivaorñ...
...Núnoe tòv iwoíav xai cou aòelq...
ieXovías*

1.7 Reasons for writing the gospel (2)

▪ The early days of the Church

In the early days of the Church's existence, there seemed to be no need for a gospel. There were many eyewitnesses to Jesus' life who could keep his memory alive and pass on the stories and teachings. They were also able to correct inaccuracies and to prevent false beliefs from taking hold.

Some of Jesus' teachings seemed to imply that the present age was about to end. The early Christians were expecting the Second Coming, when Jesus would return and all who were saved would enter the **Kingdom of God**. If the world was about to end, there would seem to be no need for a gospel.

▪ Why did a written gospel become necessary?

The delay of the Second Coming

Gradually Christians realised that the Second Coming was not imminent. This change can be seen in Paul's letters. In his earliest writings, he urged Christians to be ready for Jesus' return in judgement, which would come when they least expected it. He even advised single Christians in Corinth against getting married, as the responsibilities of marriage would distract them from their preparations for the Second Coming. In his later writings, however, there is little said about this and guidance is given on social and family life.

∞ links

For the development in Paul's beliefs about the Second Coming, and his teaching on family life, see 1 Corinthians 7:25–31; 15:51–52; Colossians 3:18–24.

The threat of heresy

As Christianity slowly expanded, converts were being made from a wide variety of cultures and religions. These converts brought with them some of the beliefs and practices of their religions, and their Greek ways of thinking. Christianity was faced with the threat of heresy, or false beliefs. This was particularly a problem in the 2nd and 3rd centuries, but even in the 1st century false beliefs were circulating. These suggested that Jesus was not really a human being and that he only seemed to die, or that someone else died in his place. There was an urgent need for such false beliefs to be shown to be wrong.

B *Dionysus – the god at the centre of a religion noted for drunken orgies*

Key terms

Kingdom of God: wherever God is honoured as king and his authority accepted. Jesus taught about the Kingdom of God both on earth and in Heaven. The rule of God.

∞ links

For more about the Kingdom of God, see Chapter 6.

A *The cult of Isis and Osiris was one of the most popular mystery religions*

The loss of eyewitnesses

As time passed, eyewitnesses grew old and died. Peter died in the persecution during the reign of Nero. Although there were many other sources of information, the evidence of eyewitnesses was especially important and needed to be preserved.

Persecution

The outbreak of persecution in Rome after the terrible fire in 64 CE and the martyrdom of both Peter and Paul made the need for a gospel more compelling. The events and significance of Jesus' life, death and resurrection needed to be committed to writing. It was not enough just to write a biography or collection of teachings. What was needed was something new: a gospel, to encourage and reassure frightened, **persecuted** Christians. Many think that Mark wrote his gospel soon after the persecution subsided, using as his basis what Peter had told him.

Key terms

Persecuted: to be treated badly, for example arrested, tortured, killed or denied rights as a result of one's beliefs.

Research activity

The Ichthus symbol

Type 'Ichthus' into a search engine. Research then explain what it means, including what each letter in the word stands for, and how early Christians used it in times of persecution. Have you seen this symbol in use today?

 The Ichthus symbol

Activity

1. a Work in pairs. Using a search engine or the websites in the Links opposite, research the fire of Rome and how it led to the persecution of Christians. You should then adopt different roles:

   Role one: Imagine that you are a Christian living in Rome when the fire breaks out. You lose everything. You are living rough, along with others who have also lost everything and who are very angry. Then you all hear a rumour that it wasn't Nero who started the fire, but Christians. Write a short story, starting from when the fire breaks out and ending with what happens to you and your family when the persecution starts. Include your impressions of how non-Christians feel about you, and how hatred sometimes turned into pity.

   Role two: Imagine you are a non-Christian in the same situation, and write the story from your viewpoint.

   b Exchange stories and discuss how you have both represented the events of the fire and persecution.

∞ links

Use the following links to help with Activity 1a:

www.bible-history.com

www.request.org.uk

www.eyewitnesstohistory.com/rome.htm

www.pbs.org/wnet/secrets/case_rome/index.html

Summary

You should now understand that the delay of the Second Coming, the rise of heresy, the death of eyewitnesses and persecution created the need for a gospel.

Study tip

Make sure that you understand why a written gospel was eventually needed.

Why were Christians unpopular?

There were a number of reasons for the unpopularity of Christians in the 1st century: some political, some social, and some based on rumour and misunderstanding. Christians were believed, wrongly, to be anti-social, immoral, and a threat in various ways.

Antisocial

Then, as now, citizenship was important. Good citizens took part in civic ceremonies, including sacrifice to the gods. As monotheists (believing in only one god), Christians could not be involved in these sacrifices. Any meat offered to them by friends and neighbours would have been sacrificed before being sold, and many Christians felt that to eat it was to recognise other gods. It must have been hard for people to understand why a sociable neighbour suddenly refused all invitations and avoided civic functions.

Immoral

All kinds of rumours spread about what went on in Christian rituals. There were accusations of ritual murder during baptism, because people are said to be 'dying' to their old life when they join the Church. Christians were also accused of cannibalism during the Eucharist, as the sacrificial death of Jesus is celebrated; and even of incest, probably because of the Christian language of universal love. Respectable Romans were scandalised by what they heard.

A threat to social and political stability

Daily life in the ancient world was dependent on slavery. Slaves worked in all kinds of jobs, and most led a miserable existence. They had no rights, were often ill treated, and were firmly controlled to prevent rebellion. Christianity appealed to slaves, with its emphasis on the dignity and equality of all human beings. Some slaves held important positions within their Christian churches. So Christianity was viewed with suspicion by many Romans.

A threat to the economy

Some cities in the Roman Empire had temples and shrines that were important centres of pilgrimage, selling statues of gods and goddesses, and lucky charms. Wherever Christianity took hold, this profitable trade was threatened.

Objectives

Understand why Christians were unpopular in the 1st century CE.

Know about the persecution of Christians by the Roman Emperor Nero.

A   *The words of the Eucharist were misunderstood by some non-Christians*

Discussion activity 🏃🏃🏃

In small groups, discuss whether the early Christians were right to refuse to take part in civic ceremonies. Do you think that being part of a community means that you should be involved in all its activities? To what extent is compromise sometimes important? Is there anything on which you would not be prepared to compromise?

Enemies of the state

The Romans allowed conquered peoples to continue to worship their own gods as long as they also showed loyalty by acknowledging the emperor as a god. The Jews were also strictly monotheist but the Romans had made a special exception in their case. With Christians, who were also not prepared to acknowledge the emperor as a god, it was different: they actively sought to make converts, so their numbers were growing, and they were already disliked. Even though Christian teaching stated that the civil authorities should be obeyed, the Romans were not prepared to make an exception for them.

■ The Neronian persecution

In 64 CE a terrible fire swept through Rome. The blame for the fire was put on the Roman Emperor Nero and he needed to find another group to blame. The unpopular Christians, already viewed with suspicion, were the obvious choice. Nero began a terrible persecution in which many died, including both Peter and Paul. This violence was limited to Rome, but it was terrifying while it lasted, and Christians realised that from then on they were likely to be harassed wherever they lived.

Research activity

The Neronian persecution

Using the website link below, read the Roman writer Tacitus' account of what happened in the Neronian persecution. Tacitus clearly hated Christians. How do you know this from what he says? Why do you think he hated them? At the end of his account, Tacitus said that many felt some pity for them. Why?

∞ links

For the fire of Rome, review the activity on page 21, if you completed it; for Tacitus' account of the persecution, see: www.eyewitnesstohistory.com/christians.htm

B   *The Colosseum in Rome – Christians were thrown to the lions here in the 2nd century as public entertainment*

Study tip

As you read Mark's Gospel, think what it was like to be a Christian in ancient Rome and why Christians were hated so much. Some of what you read in the gospel might have been intended to help those Christians.

Summary

You should now understand why Christians were seen as anti-social, immoral, enemies of the state and a threat to social stability and the economy, and why, in the persecution of 64 CE, many were killed, including Peter and Paul.

1.9 Mark's Gospel as good news for 1st-century Christians

■ Christians facing persecution

The Christians facing persecution in Rome must have been terrified and might have felt like abandoning their faith. Mark's Gospel was 'good news', and many of its stories and teachings were intended to bring encouragement, hope and the assurance of God's understanding and forgiveness.

■ The calming of the storm (Mark 4:35–41)

> #### Beliefs and teachings
>
> That day when evening came, he said to his disciples, 'Let us go over to the other side.' Leaving the crowd behind, they took him along, just as he was, in the boat. There were also other boats with him. A furious squall came up, and the waves broke over the boat, so that it was nearly swamped. Jesus was in the stern, sleeping on a cushion. The disciples woke him and said to him, 'Teacher, don't you care if we drown?'
>
> He got up, rebuked the wind and said to the waves, 'Quiet! Be still!' Then the wind died down and it was completely calm.
>
> He said to his disciples, 'Why are you so afraid? Do you still have no faith?' They were terrified and asked each other, 'Who is this? Even the wind and the waves obey him!'
>
> *Mark 4:35–41*

Objectives

Know the story of the calming of the storm, and understand how it might have helped 1st-century Christians facing hostility and persecution.

Understand the significance for Mark's readers of other incidents in Mark's Gospel.

A *Fishing boats by the shores of the Sea of Galilee*

The story's significance for 1st-century Christians in Rome

There were a number of ways in which this story was significant for 1st-century Christians. In the ancient world, violent storms were thought to be caused by demons, and Jesus' words to the storm were the same as those used in ceremonies to drive out demons ('exorcisms'). The Emperor Nero was universally hated, so Christians might well have identified demonic possession of the lake with him.

It must also have seemed as if God was asleep in their time of need, but this story showed his power to save them. Jewish Christians would have remembered Old Testament descriptions of God controlling nature. In calming the storm, Jesus demonstrated God's power over all the forces of evil.

The ship on rough seas was an early Christian symbol, representing the Church sailing over the stormy seas of life to its haven, God. This story might have reassured many that whether they lived or died, and even if their faith was shaken, they would ultimately be safe with God.

B *The Church was often depicted as a boat sailing the stormy seas of life*

Activity

1 a Read again Mark's account of the calming of the storm. Then, from memory, give an account of the story in your own words.

b Check what you have written against the text and give yourself a mark out of 5. If you have covered at least six of the main points of the story (the storm, Jesus asleep, the disciples' panic, Jesus addressing the storm, calm, Jesus' rebuke or the disciples' lack of faith, and the disciples' amazement), give yourself full marks.

Other stories in Mark's Gospel

Despair and hope

On the cross Jesus was surrounded by people mocking him. Apart from a handful of women standing at a distance, his friends were nowhere to be seen. No wonder that at the height of his agony, he cried out, 'My God, my God, why have you abandoned me?'. Yet, Mark's story of Jesus ended, not with death and despair but with an empty tomb and with the women being told that Jesus was alive. This might well have supported those early Christians in their trouble, encouraging them to believe that God would not desert them, even if at times they could not feel his presence. It would have reminded them of the hope of eternal life.

C *For many, Jesus' story ended with death and defeat*

D *For Mark, Jesus' story ended with resurrection and triumph*

Failure and forgiveness

When Jesus was arrested, all the disciples ran away and later Peter denied all knowledge of Jesus three times. Yet, when the young man told the women that Jesus was alive, he also instructed them to tell the disciples and Peter to go to Galilee, where they would see Jesus again. In other words, they were forgiven. This might have comforted those Christians who had gone back on their faith through sheer fear of what might happen. They, too, could have a new start.

∞links

Read about Jesus' death and the empty tomb, see Chapter 3; and Peter's denials, see pages 122–123.

Study tip

Mark 4:35–41 is one of the set texts. It is essential that you learn all the set texts, as in the exam you will be asked to give an account of some of them.

Summary

You should now know that Mark's Gospel told how Jesus calmed a storm, and understand that this story and others might have encouraged early Christians to trust that God was with them.

Mark's Gospel as good news for 21st-century Christians

■ Christians in the modern world

The 21st-century world is vastly different from that of the 1st century and the same is true of Christianity. In the West it has long been the established religion, and missionary activity in the 19th and 20th centuries took it, with varying degrees of success, to every continent. Nevertheless, in some countries Christians suffer harassment and persecution. This may be for being Christian or for the stand that they take against exploitation, injustice and repression. In Britain, providing they obey the laws of the land, Christians are entirely free to practise their faith and certain allowances are made for them. For example, according to the Sunday trading laws, Christian shop workers should not be penalised for refusing to work on Sundays because it is the Christian Sabbath.

However, young Christians in particular sometimes find it difficult to admit to their faith. Like those early Christians in Rome, young Christians today may be criticised for being narrow-minded and 'uncool' if they try to live up to Christian ideals and do not go along with their friends' attitudes to having the latest designer goods or casual sex. Christians might find encouragement for difficult situations in Mark's Gospel. They might look to the actions and teachings of Jesus for guidance on how to cope with hostility, whether ridicule or active persecution, and what stand to take when their government is either corrupt or passes what they consider to be unjust laws.

A *Studying Mark's Gospel may help young Christians to cope with ridicule from their peers*

■ The calming of the storm (Mark 4:35–41)

The story's significance for Christians today

Fundamentalist Christians believe that the calming of the storm happened exactly as Mark described it and that it is a nature **miracle**, portraying Jesus as the Son of God. Many Christians, however, take a

Objectives

Understand modern approaches to Mark's account of the calming of the storm.

Understand and evaluate its significance for 21st-century Christians.

Know about a modern Christian who faced hostility.

Beliefs and teachings

Remember the Sabbath day by keeping it holy … On it you shall not do any work …

Exodus 20:8, 10

∞ links

To read about Sunday as the Christian holy day, see pages 72–73; for attitudes to Christians in the 1st century, see pages 22–23.

∞ links

Re-read the set text on page 24 before working through the rest of this section.

Key terms

Miracle: an event that lies beyond normal human knowledge and understanding. It is an unexplained event with religious significance.

different view. Some think it was a story created by the Early Church to show God's power to overcome all evil. Others think something happened, but that either the storm blew over without Jesus' intervention or it was a 'miracle' of timing: as Jesus spoke, the storm just happened to end. The Sea of Galilee is noted for very violent and potentially dangerous storms that blow up without warning and then subside. Some think that Jesus spoke not to the storm but to the disciples, to calm their panic. Whatever their views, however, Christians see a deep significance in the story. As in Mark's day, many Christians facing open hostility might be inspired and encouraged to cope with their situation, believing that God will be with them.

∞ links

Read about more of Jesus' miracles in Chapters 4 and 5.

Discussion activity

1 Do you think that the story of the calming of the storm can have any meaning for Christians living in the modern world? Discuss the question in pairs or groups.

James Mawdsley

James Mawdsley is an example of a young person who was persecuted not for being a Christian but for engaging in political activities that stemmed from his Christian faith. In 1997 he went to Burma to teach in a camp for displaced persons. When the camp was attacked, he and others escaped into Thailand, returning to Burma later in the same year. He then discovered that many of the people he had been teaching had been killed or were missing. For distributing leaflets outlining the government's abuses, he was arrested, interrogated and deported. Yet again he returned to Burma, and yet again he was arrested for his protest. This time he was tortured during interrogation before being sentenced to five years in prison. He spent 99 days in solitary confinement, after which the Burmese authorities decided to deport him once again. He went back to Burma in 1999 and although he entered legally, was sentenced without trial to 17 years for illegal entry and sedition. He spent over a year in prison, and during part of that time went on hunger strike to draw attention to the plight of a Burmese activist who had spent far longer in prison. James was sustained throughout all this by his Christian faith, which told him that his cause was just. After a great deal of international pressure, he was released and returned to Britain, where he is now involved in a variety of political and religious activities.

B *James Mawdsley*

Case study

Discussion activity

2 In pairs or small groups, discuss the information about James Mawdsley. Do you think he was right to act as he did? Do you think he achieved anything, given the fact that there is still no democracy in Burma? Is it important to make a stand against injustice, whether or not it is successful?

Research activity

Oscar Romero

Investigate the life and witness of Oscar Romero. Write a short article about him, including information on what led him to make a stand against the authorities, how he made his protest, the events leading to his death, and how he continues to inspire many Christians.

Study tip

When you study the set texts, make sure that you understand how Christians in the 21st century might apply them to their lives.

Summary

You should now understand the different views Christians have regarding Mark's account of the calming of the storm, and why they all see its meaning as important. You should understand why Christians facing hostility might find support in Mark's Gospel.

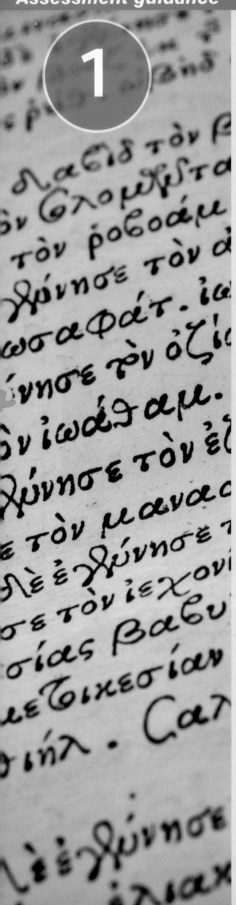

Background to Mark's Gospel – summary

For the examination, you should now be able to:

✔ understand the nature of the New Testament, the meaning of the term 'gospel' and the nature of Mark's Gospel (Mark 1:1), and know traditional views about its authorship, date and location

✔ understand about the spread of Christianity to Rome and its appeal to marginalised people in 1st-century Rome

✔ explain about primary and secondary sources of information behind Mark's Gospel and understand and evaluate different views about its authority

✔ describe the major themes running through Mark's Gospel and understand their importance for its readers

✔ understand what led to Mark's Gospel being written, particularly in relation to the Neronian persecution

✔ describe Mark's story about the calming of the storm (Mark 4:35–41) and understand its significance for Christians faced with hostility.

Sample answer

1 Write an answer to the following exam question:

Outline sources that Mark might have used for writing his gospel. *(4 marks)*

a Read the following sample answer:

> John Mark may have been the man who ran naked from Gethsemane. He lived in Jerusalem. He eventually wrote the gospel.

b With a partner, discuss the sample answer. This is a very brief answer. What details are missing? How could it be improved?

c What mark would you give this answer out of 4? Look at the mark scheme in the Introduction on page 7 (AO1). What are the reasons for the mark you have given?

Practice questions

I'M A CHRISTIAN, TOO, AND SO IS MY OLDER SISTER. SHE'S PREGNANT AND WE DISCUSSED WHETHER SHE SHOULD HAVE AN ABORTION AS SHE AND HER HUSBAND WANT TO BE MORE FINANCIALLY SETTLED BEFORE HAVING A BABY. THERE WAS NOTHING IN JESUS' TEACHING IN MARK'S GOSPEL TO GUIDE US.

I'M A CHRISTIAN. MARK'S GOSPEL HELPS ME PUT UP WITH THE TEASING I GET FOR GOING TO CHURCH.

I'M NOT A CHRISTIAN BUT SOME OF JESUS' TEACHING THAT I'VE READ IN MARK'S GOSPEL MAKES GOOD SENSE TO ME.

1   What does the word 'gospel' mean?   *(1 mark)*

2   Give two reasons why Mark wrote a gospel.   *(2 marks)*

3   Explain how the story of the calming of the storm might have helped 1st-century Christians face up to persecution.   *(3 marks)*

> **Study tip** Question 3 asks you to explain the story of the calming of the storm in one particular way. Do not describe the whole story, just use relevant bits to show how it might have helped 1st-century Christians facing persecution.

4   'Mark's Gospel is 2,000 years old. To help them live Christian lives, people today need something more up to date.' Do you agree? Give reasons for your answer, showing that you have thought about more than one point of view.   *(6 marks)*

> **Study tip** Remember to use the stimulus material to help you with answers to questions. The picture on this page should give you ideas for the fourth question.

2 Jesus' ministry

2.1 Roman rule in Palestine

Roman policy in conquered lands

The Romans wanted peace and stability in their empire. Trustworthy rulers of conquered lands were left in power. Troublesome areas became provinces of the Roman Empire, and those on the borders of the Empire had governors appointed by the emperor and his advisers. They were closely watched for problems.

Palestine

Palestine was the Roman name for the land the Jews have always referred to as Israel. The Romans took over Palestine in 63 BCE, knowing it would be a difficult land to govern. The Jews were well known for their civil wars. Palestine was also right on the edge of the Roman Empire. Just to the east was the powerful Parthian Empire, from which the Romans feared attacks through the unstable lands of Palestine. The Romans needed a strong ruler for Palestine whose loyalty to Rome could be trusted. Eventually, Herod was appointed. Loyal to Rome beyond question, he claimed to practise the Jewish faith, though he was not Jewish by birth. He brought peace to his kingdom, but the Jews detested him. Not only was he a foreigner, he was also corrupt and ruthless. When he died in 4 BCE, his kingdom was divided between three of his sons, although one who ruled badly was replaced with a governor.

Map A shows the political structure of Palestine during Jesus' ministry, together with places mentioned in Mark's Gospel. Galilee and Peraea were ruled by Herod's son, Antipas. It was Antipas who arrested and executed John the Baptist. The largely Gentile territories to the north-east were ruled by Philip, another of Herod's sons. It was during a journey in this territory that Peter declared Jesus to be the Messiah. The provinces of Judaea, Samaria and Idumaea were ruled by a governor, Pontius Pilate. It was Pilate who sentenced Jesus to death.

∞ links

For John the Baptist, see pages 38–39; for Jesus' trial before Pilate, see pages 60–61.

For John the Baptist, see pages 38–39; for Jesus' trial before Pilate, see pages 60–61.

Objectives

Understand how the Romans governed the lands they conquered and how this applied to Palestine at the time of Jesus.

Understand the effect political issues might have had on the lives of people in Palestine in the time of Jesus.

Use this background information to deepen your understanding of Jesus' ministry.

A *Palestine in the time of Jesus*

Activity

1 Answer the following questions without using any books or notes to help you. Then check your answers in the text above.

a How did the Romans try to ensure peace within their empire?

b Who ruled Galilee after the death of Herod?

c Who governed Judaea during the lifetime of Jesus?

d Why was it so important for the Romans to try to maintain peace in Palestine?

Continual unrest in Palestine

The Romans compromised with the Jews to keep the peace in Palestine. The Jews – who believed in one god – did not have to worship the emperor or perform military service, as both of these would have recognised the emperor as a god. The Roman army carried standards, flags which represented the different legions of the army. It was agreed that these were not to be brought into Jerusalem, because the presence of the Temple made Jerusalem a holy city, and the standards displayed images that were offensive to Jews.

B *Roman standards could not be brought into Jerusalem*

Nevertheless, throughout the lifetime of Jesus there were continual uprisings. The Jews resented being ruled by foreigners, and the atmosphere was always very strained. In particular, at Passover (the annual festival celebrating the Jews' ancestors' deliverance from slavery) there was the possibility of serious trouble. Jerusalem was crowded with pilgrims from all over the Mediterranean world, and the sheer numbers of people created tension. As the Jews celebrated their deliverance by God from slavery, they would have been reminded that they were **not** free, and many believed that the Messiah would come at Passover time to liberate them. In order to keep control, the Roman governor always moved from his headquarters at Caesarea to Jerusalem during Passover.

Activities

2 The Jews based their lives on the Ten Commandments, which are listed in Exodus 20:2–17. Look up this passage in a Bible or on the internet. Now explain, with reference to the relevant Commandments, why the Jews could not acknowledge the Roman emperor as a god.

3 Pilate once broke the rule and allowed his soldiers to bring their standards into Jerusalem. His action led to riots by the Jews. Explain why.

4 Why would Pilate have been especially on the lookout for any trouble at Passover time?

Discussion activity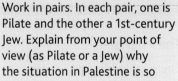

Work in pairs. In each pair, one is Pilate and the other a 1st-century Jew. Explain from your point of view (as Pilate or a Jew) why the situation in Palestine is so difficult and unfair for you. Use the information on these pages to support your point of view.

Study tip

Although you will not be asked a question on the political situation in Palestine during the ministry of Jesus, being aware of it will help you to a deeper understanding, especially of the final days of Jesus' life.

Summary

You should now understand some important background to Jesus' life and work: that Palestine under Roman rule was politically very sensitive; that Jesus' home province was governed by Antipas; and that Judaea was governed by Pontius Pilate.

Introduction

Mark's Gospel refers to a number of Jewish religious or political groups in 1st-century Palestine. You will not be examined on these, but understanding their roles and beliefs will help you to understand how they came into conflict with Jesus.

The Sadducees

Most of the Sadducees were priests, mainly concerned with the Temple and the worship that went on in it, and with little interest in ordinary Jews. They had a very conservative approach to religion, resisting change and rejecting any beliefs that could not be found in the written Law or Torah (the first five books of the Jewish scriptures). They did not believe in life after death or the idea of a Messiah.

The Sanhedrin

This was the supreme council of the Jews, consisting mainly of Sadducees. It had 71 members, the most important being the high priest. During Jesus' ministry, the high priest was Caiaphas. All high priests were appointed by the Romans, reminding the council that it owed its power to the emperor. The Sanhedrin oversaw the running of the Temple. It was also a law court, able to try capital cases. However, cases involving crimes for which Jewish law prescribed death were referred to the Roman governor. To keep its privileged position, the Sanhedrin had to be seen to support the Romans and watch out for rebellions.

A   *The Western Wall – the only part of the 1st-century Temple that is still standing*

The Pharisees

There were Pharisees in every town and village in Palestine and in every Jewish community throughout the Empire. Helping to run the synagogues, they were forward-looking in their ideas and were often highly respected by other Jews. They thought that the Kingdom of God would come when all Jews kept the Torah, and so observed it very strictly. They also awaited the coming of a descendant of King David as the Messiah. The Pharisees disliked the Romans but opposed any use of violence to overthrow them.

The scribes

Sometimes referred to in the New Testament as 'doctors of the law', scribes were experts in the written Law or Torah. Over the years, they created many extra rules, known as the oral tradition, to help Jews understand exactly what the Law required. Many were Pharisees, and some were rabbis, teaching in synagogues and in the Temple courtyard.

B   *Rabbis are still seen as experts in the meaning of the written Law*

Zealots

Often thought of, wrongly, as a political group, Zealots were in fact deeply religious people. They differed from the Pharisees only in their belief that the Messiah would be a warrior figure who would overthrow Roman rule by force. They were responsible for many uprisings.

Herodians

Herodians were the supporters of Herod Antipas and Rome, and their concerns were political: to keep the Herod family in power. Few would have been Jewish by birth, or by preference. Antipas, though brought up a Jew, showed no religious commitment.

In conflict with Jesus

Throughout his ministry, Jesus clashed with the scribes and Pharisees over a number of issues. Until his protest in the Temple, he had few encounters with the Sadducees, but after his protest, they were determined to kill him. It was the Sanhedrin who had him arrested and who handed him over to Pilate after conducting their own trial. There are a few references to Zealots in the gospel. At least one of Jesus' disciples was a member of this group. It might have been Zealot ideals that made Judas betray Jesus. Mark also referred to the Herodians. Although the Pharisees, in particular, disliked the Herodians, on two occasions they joined forces against Jesus.

∞ links

Read more: Caiaphas, Sanhedrin, Sadducees, Chapters 3 and 5; scribes and Pharisees, Chapters 4, 5 and 6; Zealots, Chapter 3; Herodians, Chapter 5.

Activities

1. Why do you think the Romans allowed the Sanhedrin so much power?
2. How did the Romans ensure that the Sanhedrin knew who was really in charge?
3. Explain briefly the differing attitudes towards Rome shown by the Sanhedrin, the Pharisees, the Zealots and the Herodians. A chart or table might be the clearest way of setting out this information.
4. Why do you think the Pharisees hated the Herodians?

Discussion activity

After you have completed the questions, look again at your answer to question 3. Then get into groups of four, in which each person should take the role of a member of one of the groups listed in question 3. Discuss your different attitudes to Rome and the reasons for the differences. Then each of you summarise the most important thing your group believes in.

Summary

You should now understand that there were many different religious groups in 1st-century Palestine, each with its own distinctive views. You should know what their views were, and begin to see how they came into conflict with Jesus.

Study tip

You will not be asked specific questions on these different groups, but understanding what they believed in will help you understand the stories about Jesus, and why he so often came into conflict with them.

The Temple

The magnificent **Temple** that was standing in Jerusalem throughout Jesus' life was built by Herod in an attempt to please his subjects and convince them that he practised their faith. God was believed to be especially present in the Temple. The building was structured like most temples in the ancient world. Entry was limited, and the further you entered, the more restrictions there were.

A *This model shows how the Temple might have looked*

The Holy of Holies: the Jews believed that God was especially present in this innermost part of the Temple, separated from the rest of the Temple by a curtain.

The Western Wall: the only part of the Temple still standing today.

The Altar of Sacrifice: sacrifice was seen as the ultimate way to make contact with God, and was used as a way of asking God to forgive sins, or to offer thanksgiving.

The Court of the Gentiles, or Temple Court: the only part of the Temple where Gentiles were admitted for prayer. Here, sacrificial animals were sold and money was exchanged for the payment of the Temple tax.

The Court of Israel: where Jewish men went to pray and offer sacrifices.

The Court of Priests: where the priests, assisted by Levites, sacrificed animals and birds on an altar.

The Court of Women: women were not allowed to go further into the Temple than here.

The Treasury: where people made donations.

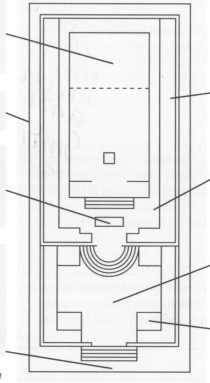

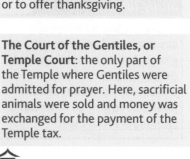

B *A plan of Herod's Temple in Jerusalem*

Activity

The Temple and the activities that took place in it are referred to several times in Mark's Gospel. Read and then copy the table. The first column lists a number of gospel references. Look these up, and then summarise the information given about the Temple in the second column. All but one of these are set texts, so it is important to know and understand them.

References to the Temple in Mark's Gospel	
Gospel reference	**Content of reference**
11:15–18	
12:32–34	
12:41–44	
13:1–2 (not set text)	
14:48–49	
14:57–59	
15:29–30	
15:37–38	

▊ Synagogues

Jews also worshipped in synagogues, which were to be found throughout the Roman Empire. As with synagogues today, Jews went there on the Sabbath for worship based on prayer, psalms, reading the Torah (the written Law), and teaching including discussion. But the synagogues were more than just places for worship. They also provided meeting points for the Jewish community, offering a place for education and study. The Pharisees played a central part in the running of synagogues, which had a number of officials. In Mark's Gospel there are several references to occasions when Jesus attended the synagogue.

C   *Reading the Torah is an important part of synagogue worship*

⚭ links

Read more about these institutions in Jesus' ministry: the Temple, Chapters 3, 5 and 6; the synagogues, Chapter 5.

Summary

You should now know and understand the layout and purpose of Herod's Temple in Jerusalem, and the purposes of synagogues.

Jesus' ministry

Many scholars think that Jesus' ministry took place between the years 27–30 CE. These two pages give a very brief overview of Mark's coverage of Jesus' life. This coverage falls into four main parts. Some of the events referred to here will be covered in detail in the rest of this chapter; others will be studied in later chapters. It is important, however, to have a clear overview of the whole ministry so that you can put the individual stories into context.

Events that led to the start of Jesus' ministry

The stories around Jesus' birth that Christians commemorate at Christmas and Epiphany are found only in the gospels of Matthew and Luke. Mark's Gospel gives no information about the life of Jesus before his baptism, but we do know (from Mark 6:3) that he came from Nazareth in the province of Galilee and that he was a carpenter.

A *Nazareth today*

After the introductory verse to his gospel, stating that it is about 'Jesus Christ, the Son of God', Mark moves straight on to the ministry of John the Baptist, which led directly to the baptism of Jesus. He then goes on to tell about Jesus' time of temptation in the wilderness. According to Mark, three events led to the start of Jesus' ministry: his baptism, his temptation and the arrest of John the Baptist.

Galilean ministry

For most of his ministry, Jesus travelled around Galilee, proclaiming the Kingdom of God through teaching and healing. He occasionally went into Gentile territory, possibly to avoid the attention of Galilee's Roman governor, Antipas. His teaching was at first directed to ordinary people, who came in crowds to hear him. Mark recorded two events that then affected both what he taught and how he taught it: the discussion about his identity at Caesarea Philippi and the transfiguration.

Objectives

Gain an overview of the contents of Mark's Gospel.

∞ **links**

Jesus' baptism, temptation, conversation at Caesarea Philippi and the transfiguration are covered later in this chapter and in Chapter 4.

B *Jesus spent much of his time preaching and healing around the Sea of Galilee*

Journey from Caesarea Philippi to Jerusalem

From Caesarea Philippi, Jesus made his way back to Galilee and then on to Jerusalem. At this point, the mood of the gospel's account changes. Only two healings are recorded and Jesus' teaching becomes largely directed at his disciples, focusing on his imminent suffering and the demands that discipleship would make on them.

The last week in and around Jerusalem

The last week of Jesus' life and the story of the empty tomb take up more than a quarter of the chapters in Mark's Gospel. The original gospel ended at 16:8, but there are now further verses in the final chapter, which were probably added to the gospel in the 2nd century.

These final chapters are very carefully structured. They contain:

- Jesus' entry into Jerusalem and the incident in the Temple
- challenges to Jesus
- teaching on the fall of Jerusalem and the end of the age
- the Passion story
- the story of the empty tomb.

⬭ links

For more on Jesus' final week in Jerusalem, see Chapter 3 and 5 pages 98–101.

C   *Mark's Gospel ends with the story of the empty tomb*

Activity

1   After reading these pages, answer the following questions from memory. When you have finished, use the book to check your answers.

   a   When did Jesus' ministry probably take place?
   b   Which three events led to the start of Jesus' ministry?
   c   In what two ways did Jesus proclaim the Kingdom of God?
   d   What two events brought his Galilean ministry to an end?
   e   After these two events, Jesus concentrated on teaching his disciples. What were the two main themes of that teaching?
   f   Name two events that took place in the last week of Jesus' life.

Summary

You should now understand that Mark's Gospel covers Jesus' ministry in four parts: baptism and temptation; public ministry in Galilee, Caesarea Philippi and the transfiguration; teaching of the disciples and the journey to Jerusalem; and the final week in Jerusalem.

2.5   Jesus' baptism

Introduction

The **baptism** of Jesus is a key event in Mark's Gospel, as it marked the end of Jesus' years as a carpenter and the start of his new life as a travelling teacher. Some Christians have tried to imagine what went on in Jesus' mind in the earlier years of his life. But as far as Mark was concerned, the first really significant event in Jesus' life was his baptism.

John the Baptist

Mark's Gospel portrays John, who was a Jewish preacher, as fulfilling the Jews' belief that the prophet Elijah would return to prepare the Jews for the Messiah's coming. John carried out baptism by total immersion in the river Jordan as a sign of repentance, the forgiveness of sins and a new beginning. It was seen as a preparation for the coming Kingdom of God.

Jesus' baptism (Mark 1:9–11)

> ### Beliefs and teachings
>
> At that time Jesus came from Nazareth in Galilee and was baptised by John in the Jordan. As Jesus was coming up out of the water, he saw heaven being torn open and the Spirit descending on him like a dove. And a voice came from heaven: 'You are my Son, whom I love; with you I am well pleased.'
>
> *Mark* 1:9–11

An explanation of the symbolism

According to Mark's Gospel, Jesus had a deep religious experience at his baptism. To help his readers understand the significance of this event, Mark used a number of Old Testament symbols.

The heavens opening

Jesus' vision of the heavens opening symbolised the presence of God. In the Old Testament book of Isaiah, God was asked to open the heavens.

The dove

Mark said that the Holy Spirit descended on Jesus like a dove. This is an important image: in one Jewish commentary on the Old Testament, the voice of the Spirit was likened to the voice of the turtle dove. In another commentary, on Genesis 1:2, the Spirit of God was said to be brooding on the waters like a dove. Some Christians think of the dove as a symbol of peace. They interpret this imagery to mean that Jesus experienced the peace of God in his heart.

The voice from heaven

Finally, Mark referred to a voice from heaven. He wanted to avoid any reference to God that might suggest he was human, but he also wanted to make it clear that Jesus was receiving both direct divine approval and the confirmation that he was God's beloved Son.

Objectives

Know and understand Mark's account of the baptism of Jesus.

Understand the significance of this event for Jesus and for Christians.

Key terms

Baptism: in Mark's Gospel, John the Baptist used baptism as a way of washing away sins in readiness for the coming of the Messiah. He also baptised Jesus, though this was not connected with washing away of sin.

A   *The river Jordan*

> ### Beliefs and teachings
>
> Oh, that you would rend the heavens and come down, that the mountains would tremble before you!
>
> *Isaiah* 64:1

B   *The dove – one of the symbols used in Mark's account of Jesus' baptism*

⚭ links

For more on this story in relation to the title Son of God, see pages 90–91.

Activities

1. How did John's baptism convey the idea of a new beginning for those who came to be baptised by him?
2. Mark's account of Jesus' baptism is full of symbolism. Which part of the story do you see as being the most important? Explain your opinion.

C *21st-century believers being baptised in the river Jordan*

The significance of his baptism for Jesus

It is impossible to know exactly what his baptism meant for Jesus, but Mark's Gospel presents it as a turning point in his life. From an unknown Galilean beginning, Jesus became a public and highly controversial figure. The baptism provided the confirmation or assurance that Jesus was the Son of God. Jesus saw himself as the Messiah, called to proclaim the good news of God's Kingdom.

The significance of Jesus' baptism for Christians

Mark did not explain why Jesus came for baptism. According to Christian belief, Jesus was sinless, and so there was no need for forgiveness. Christians tend to assume that he wished to be associated with those who came to be cleansed of sin through baptism, and that this demonstrates his humility. At the same time, what happened at Jesus' baptism indicates his authority, coming from his unique relationship with God. Most Christians practise the rite of baptism. They understand it as initiation into the Church, as symbolising membership of the Kingdom of God and as following Jesus' example.

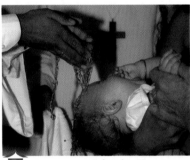

D *21st-century infant baptism*

Extension activity

Read Mark's account of John's ministry. How did John compare himself and his ministry with that of Jesus?

links

The ministry of John the Baptist is covered in Mark 1:2–8.

William Carey 1761–1834

William Carey had a very basic education in a charity school before becoming a shoemaker in Northampton. While he was an apprentice he did something dishonest that made him ask God for forgiveness. From that moment on, his life changed, and he always tried to do what God wanted. By the end of his life, the former shoemaker was a professor in India, and had translated the Bible into many different languages. Use the websites in the Links opposite to find out more about how his life changed.

Case study

links

For information on William Carey, see www.request.org.uk. From the main site, click 'History' then 'Georgians'.

Also, see www.thecareyexperience.co.uk.

Summary

You should now understand that Jesus' baptism led to his Messianic mission, that Mark's account uses Old Testament symbols to present Jesus as the Son of God, and that baptism is the rite of initiation into the Christian Church.

Study tip

You will need to understand why Mark considered the baptism of Jesus to be such an important event.

2.6 Jesus' temptation

Introduction

Immediately after his baptism, Jesus went into the Judaean desert, an area around the Dead Sea that was rocky and infertile. Jesus might have gone there to think about his future. While there, his commitment to God was tested by Satan, the evil force that tempts people, also known as the Devil.

The temptation (Mark 1:12–13)

An explanation of the symbolism

As with the baptism, the two sentences in Mark's Gospel relating this event contain a wealth of meaning.

Driven out

According to Mark, Jesus was sent or driven out; Mark also uses the Greek verb elsewhere in this gospel for exorcism. This points to the seriousness of the temptation in the desert.

Forty days

There are many Old Testament references to 40 days, such as the time Moses spent on Mt Sinai when he received the Law, but it was often used simply as a round figure meaning a long time.

Satan and the wild animals

By the time of Jesus, Jews thought of Satan as an evil power – in opposition to God and trying to lead humans astray. Wild animals represented opposition to God and were sometimes identified with demons. So these two images point to Jesus' faith being severely tested.

Angels

In the Old Testament, angels were messengers of God who brought his help to good people in difficulties. On this occasion, they represented the support that God gave Jesus in the desert.

Objectives

Know and understand Mark's account of the temptation of Jesus.

Understand its possible significance for Jesus and for Christians.

Beliefs and teachings

At once the Spirit sent him out into the desert, and he was in the desert for forty days, being tempted by Satan. He was with the wild animals, and angels attended him.

Mark 1:12–13

A *The Judaean desert*

B *Christ in the desert, attended by angels*

The meaning of the event for Jesus

According to Mark, Jesus was tested by Satan. Perhaps Satan was trying to shake Jesus' belief in his status as the Messiah and in his unique relationship with God. Jesus triumphed over this attempt, however. He returned from the desert ready to start his ministry in Galilee, thanks to his awareness of God's support. When he heard of John's arrest, he began proclaiming that God's Kingdom was near and urging Jews to repent and believe the good news.

The meaning of the event for Christians

Mark probably intended to show the temptation as further reinforcing the unique status and authority of Jesus. He was, indeed, the Son of God, as shown at the baptism, and he had authority even over Satan. Mark wanted Christians to read the gospel with this in mind, even though Jesus' powers were often hidden, and revealed only to those with faith.

C *Bible study groups are common during Lent so that Christians can help each other to grow closer to God*

Christians have, for centuries, remembered Jesus' temptation in the season of Lent. During Lent they might fast, take on a particular task, or give something up. In doing so, they are hoping to increase their self-discipline and devotion to God. Christians suffering hostility or other difficulties in their lives might be encouraged to trust that God will be there to support them, as he supported Jesus. In a time of persecution, this message might be especially important to Christians.

Activities

1 Why might Mark have said Jesus was sent or driven into the desert by the Spirit rather than simply saying that Jesus went into the desert?

2 Explain how Mark's account of the temptation reinforces the message of Jesus' baptism.

Extension activity

Jesus was further tempted on many occasions. In pairs, create a table with three columns headed 'Text', 'What Jesus might have been tempted to do' and 'How Jesus dealt with the temptation'. In the first column, write each of the following references: Mark 3:2; 6:30–33; 8:31–32; 14:41–43; 15:3–4. As you enter each reference, look it up in your Bible and discuss what Jesus might have been tempted to do and how he dealt with the temptation. Then fill in the other two columns with your ideas.

∞ links

For help with the extension activity, see pages 42–43, 56–57, 60–61, 78–79 and 96–97.

Study tip

Stories like Jesus' baptism and temptation can be hard for 21st-century non-Jews to understand. If you find the symbolism difficult, focus on the meaning of these events for Jesus' ministry and for Christians who read Mark's Gospel.

Summary

You should now understand that Mark's account of the temptation reinforces the authority of Jesus, and is important because it precedes the start of Jesus' ministry. You should understand how Christians might take encouragement and comfort from Jesus' victory over temptation.

2.7 Caesarea Philippi (1)

Introduction

Caesarea Philippi was not in Galilee, but in a Gentile region ruled by Philip, who had named the town after himself and the emperor. Its modern name is Banias. It was here that Jesus had an important conversation with his disciples.

Caesarea Philippi (Mark 8:27–33)

Beliefs and teachings

Jesus and his disciples went on to the villages around Caesarea Philippi. On the way he asked them, 'Who do people say I am?'

They replied, 'Some say John the Baptist; others say Elijah; and still others, one of the prophets.'

'But what about you?' he asked. 'Who do you say I am?'

Peter answered, 'You are the Christ.'

Jesus warned them not to tell anyone about him.

He then began to teach them that the Son of Man must suffer many things and be rejected by the elders, chief priests and teachers of the law, and that he must be killed and after three days rise again. He spoke plainly about this, and Peter took him aside and began to rebuke him.

But when Jesus turned and looked at his disciples, he rebuked Peter. 'Get behind me, Satan!' he said. 'You do not have in mind the things of God, but the things of men.'

Mark 8:27–33

The significance of this text

This text is important because it contains the first recorded recognition of Jesus as Messiah. When Peter declared, 'You are the Christ', Jesus did not deny it, but ordered his disciples to keep it a secret. This key text also includes the first of the Passion predictions, in which Jesus predicts his imminent suffering and death. Jesus here referred to himself as the Son of Man, saying that after much suffering he would be rejected by the Sanhedrin and killed, but that he would be raised back to life. He then rebuked Peter for thinking as a man and not remembering God's purpose, when Peter tried to tell him this must be wrong. He referred to Peter as Satan: Peter was wrong in tempting him to take an easier path as Messiah.

Objectives

Know the conversation that took place on the way to Caesarea Philippi.

Understand its importance, both as a turning point in Jesus' ministry and for Jesus himself.

A *The Banias river today. Banias is the modern name for Caesarea Philippi*

∞ links

For more about this incident in relation to the titles Messiah and Son of Man, read pages 84–85 and pages 88–89.

Activities

1. Jesus may have left Galilee to avoid arrest but he predicted that it would happen at some point. Why might he have wanted to avoid arrest at this time?

2. Why did Jesus not want people to know he was the Messiah? (If you are not sure of the answer, you might find it helpful to look at pages 84–85).

3. What did Jesus say about his future in this text?

1 In pairs, make up a role play, imagining how Peter might have replied to Jesus' rebuke, and what else might have been said. You might decide to imagine Peter sticking to his view, or alternatively as accepting what Jesus said even though it went against everything he had always believed. Whichever you choose, you also have to imagine how Jesus might have responded.

The importance of this event for Jesus

The conversation that took place on the way to Caesarea Philippi marked a real turning point, or **watershed**, in Jesus' ministry. From this point on, almost everything Jesus said and did pointed to his imminent and inevitable death.

Before

Until this point in Mark's Gospel, Jesus' ministry was mostly in the public eye, consisting of teaching and healing. He did encounter hostility in Galilee. Mark notes that the Pharisees and Herodians joined forces to plot his death and that Antipas thought he was another John the Baptist (and would therefore have to be killed, like John). Maybe this is why Jesus moved in and out of Galilee. But for much of the time, the atmosphere was apparently positive and people were eager to listen to him.

After

Everything changed after Caesarea Philippi and the atmosphere became 'darker'. Passing through Galilee, Jesus did not want anyone to know he was there, so that he could focus on teaching the disciples. That teaching included many predictions of his suffering and death and this made his companions very uneasy. It is clear from what he said in this passage that Jesus saw his coming suffering as God's will for him. He said that the Son of Man **must** suffer and be killed. This is often referred to as the divine 'must'.

Watershed: something which happens that changes the course of history or someone's life.

Make sure that you understand how this incident was a watershed or turning point, separating Jesus' Galilean ministry from his journey to Jerusalem and his final week there.

4 Read the following passages from Mark's Gospel: 8:31; 9:12, 31; 10:33–34, 45. Create a table with two columns. In the first column put the references, and in the second summarise in your own words what Jesus said. Highlight the first and the last, as these are both set texts for study.

2 Jesus said that the Son of Man must suffer. Does this mean he believed that his fate was fixed and that there is no such thing as free will? What do you think about fate and free will? Do you think we do have free choice, or do you think our futures are all mapped out in advance by some other force: God, the stars, or fate? Discuss these questions in small groups and then report back to the class in a plenary session.

Summary

You should now understand the significance of the conversation at Caesarea Philippi. When Peter declared Jesus to be the Messiah, Jesus ordered him not to tell anyone. Jesus called himself the Son of Man, and made the first prediction of his suffering and death.

Caesarea Philippi (Mark 8:27–33)

The importance of this event for the disciples

When Peter declared Jesus to be the Messiah, he was probably speaking on behalf of all 12 disciples. They must have discussed the identity of Jesus. To give up their homes and jobs to follow him suggests they truly believed he was sent by God. They still did not understand, however, how Jesus interpreted being the Messiah, and were still thinking in terms of glory for him and themselves. Jesus' final comment shows how much Peter and the others had to learn. Caesarea Philippi marked the start of an intensive period of teaching, about Jesus' imminent suffering and about the demands that discipleship would make of them. On several occasions Jesus had to rebuke the disciples and there are a number references to them being afraid.

The healing of a blind man and Caesarea Philippi

Although it is not a set passage, it is worth looking at Mark's account of the healing of a blind man at Bethsaida. Many scholars think Mark intended this story as a pointer to the importance of the Caesarea Philippi story. The table below sets out the parallels between the two.

A　*Parallels between the healing of a blind man and Caesarea Philippi*

Feature	Blind man at Bethsaida	Caesarea Philippi
About 'sight'	Physical sight	Spiritual 'sight'
Out of the public eye	Jesus took the man out of Bethsaida	On the way to Caesarea Philippi
Two-fold structure	The healing action had to be performed twice	Two questions were put to the disciples
Partial 'sight' the first time	The man's vision was blurred	The disciples at first said that people thought Jesus was John, Elijah etc.
Full 'sight' the second time	The man saw clearly	Peter said, 'You are the Messiah'
The Messianic Secret	The man was told not to go to Bethsaida	Jesus warned the disciples to tell no one

The importance of this event for Christians

Much of the importance of this text concerns the titles Messiah and Son of Man, but there is another key issue. Jesus did not say that the Son of Man **would** suffer, but that he **must** suffer. Christians understand this to mean that his suffering and death were part of God's purpose. This was a central aspect of the good news that Jesus brought. That good news included Jesus' life as well as his teaching. Those 1st-century Christians who were facing persecution were encouraged to think that their sufferings also had purpose, even if they could not understand it. Many Christians today who suffer try to see their suffering in a similar light.

Objectives

Understand the importance of the conversation at Caesarea Philippi for Jesus' disciples and for Christians.

◯◯links

Read the text of Mark 8:27–33 on page 42 before continuing with these pages.

◯◯links

Read the story of the healing of a blind man in Mark 8:22–26.

B　*Jesus healing the blind man*

◯◯links

The meaning of the titles Messiah and Son of Man are considered in Chapter 4.

Discussion activity

Karl Marx said that religion was 'the opium of the people'. Many people view religion as a kind of escapism, a refusal to face reality. They think that Christians accept suffering because they believe God has everything under control and that they will be rewarded for their attitude after death. What do you think? Do you think any good can come out of suffering and that it ever has a purpose?

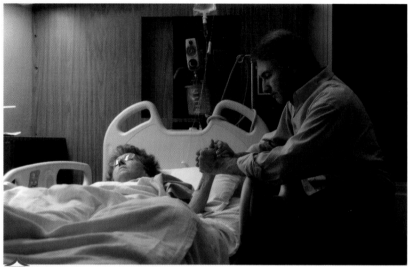

C *Christians try to see some purpose in suffering*

> He or she has led me a merry dance into the torture chamber and out, into the convent and out, and then through twenty years of the most satisfying work a woman could wish for. Now I have emerged into a sunlit meadow and I feel God's love like the sun on my back. I have no idea what joy or suffering the future may bring but I am ready for either.
>
> *Sheila Cassidy, Made for Laughter*

Sheila Cassidy

Case study

After training as a doctor in the 1960s, Sheila Cassidy went to work in Chile. A political coup took place while she was there and any opposition to the new regime was ruthlessly dealt with. So when in 1975 she gave medical care to a government opponent, she was arrested and kept in custody without trial. During that time she was repeatedly tortured. Her way of survival was to say to God, 'Do with me as you wish'. She was eventually released and returned to the UK. It took her many years to recover from her ordeal, and for part of that time she lived in a monastery and a convent. She eventually returned to medical work in a hospice and in palliative care. She is involved with charities and is an author. An extract from one of her books describes how she sees God at work throughout her life.

Study tip

The miracles in Mark's Gospel always have a deeper meaning. They connect to Jesus' teaching about himself and about the Kingdom of God. When you read these stories, try to be aware of those links.

Research activity

Irina Ratushinskaya

Find out about Irina Ratushinskaya's life by typing her name into a search engine. Make brief notes on her life, including why she was imprisoned, how she was treated and how she was enabled to survive. Note particularly what she wrote in relation to her awareness of God's love. You might want to use the case study on Sheila Cassidy as a model for your notes.

Summary

You should now know how, at Caesarea Philippi, the disciples through Peter recognised Jesus as the Messiah but did not understand that he must suffer. Christians try to develop a positive attitude to suffering even if they cannot understand its purpose.

Introduction

Peter, James and John seem to have formed an inner circle of disciples. It was six days after Caesarea Philippi that Jesus took these three up a high mountain and they witnessed the events known as the transfiguration.

The transfiguration (Mark 9:2–8)

Beliefs and teachings

After six days Jesus took Peter, James and John with him and led them up a high mountain, where they were all alone. There he was transfigured before them. His clothes became dazzling white, whiter than anyone in the world could bleach them. And there appeared before them Elijah and Moses, who were talking with Jesus.

Peter said to Jesus, 'Rabbi, it is good for us to be here. Let us put up three shelters – one for you, one for Moses and one for Elijah.' (He did not know what to say, they were so frightened.)

Then a cloud appeared and enveloped them, and a voice came from the cloud: 'This is my Son, whom I love. Listen to him!'

Suddenly, when they looked around, they no longer saw anyone with them except Jesus.

Mark 9:2–8

An explanation of the symbolism

Like the baptism and the temptation stories, the story of the transfiguration is rich in symbolic meaning.

The Son of God

The dazzling whiteness of Jesus' clothes signified that he was more than just a man. This is reinforced at the end by God's confirmation of him as his beloved (only) Son. The first words spoken by God were identical to those recorded at Jesus' baptism and the cloud indicated God's presence.

Moses and Elijah

Moses and Elijah were two of the most important Old Testament figures. Moses was said to be the greatest of the prophets, who liberated the slaves from Egypt and received the Torah, the Jews' most holy scriptures. He is seen here as a symbol of Jewish law. Elijah was a great prophet who experienced God's presence. Jews thought that he would return to prepare them for the coming of the Messiah. When Jews celebrate Passover, Elijah's cup is on the table and the door is opened in case he should return. He is seen here as a representative of the prophets. The appearance of these two pointed to Jesus as the fulfilment of the Old Testament. In other words, the teaching he gave at Caesarea Philippi was in accordance with God's will.

Objectives

Know Mark's account of Jesus' transfiguration.

Understand the symbolism in the story.

Understand the importance of the event for Jesus, for the three disciples and for Christians.

Key terms

Transfiguration: an incident in the New Testament when Jesus was lit up by divine light, through which the divinity of Jesus was revealed (Mark 9:2–9).

A *The church on Mt Tabor – believed to be the mountain site of the transfiguration*

B *Passover meal: Elijah's cup*

The shelters

The shelters suggested by Peter might just have been his way of wanting to show respect. Or Mark might have wanted his readers to think of the sacred tent, used for prayer during the wilderness wanderings, or of the tents in which the Israelites lived during that time, and which Jews still remember at the festival of Sukkoth.

∞ links

For the sacred tent used for prayer and the tents used in the wilderness, see Exodus 33:7–11 and Leviticus 23:42–43.

Activities

1. Without using any books or these pages, explain the meaning of the transfiguration, jotting down the key points that you can remember.

2. Read again Mark 9:2–8 and the explanation given here of the symbolism in this text. Then check your work against what you have read and give yourself a mark out of 5. Award yourself full marks if you have explained three of the symbolic details in the story. If you have only told the story, without referring to the symbolism, the maximum mark is 2.

C *A rabbi celebrating Sukkoth*

The importance of the transfiguration for Jesus

Peter's strong rejection of his reference to suffering and death at Caesarea Philippi might have been a real temptation for Jesus: was this really what God wanted? The transfiguration must have reassured Jesus that he was following the right path. It led directly into the next phase of his ministry.

Its importance for Peter, James and John

When Peter rejected the idea of a suffering Messiah, it was probably because it went against everything he had always believed. It is very likely that James and John agreed with him. What the three disciples saw was a vision of Jesus in glory. It confirmed for them that he was neither Moses nor Elijah, as some people thought, but the Son of God. Most importantly, the voice ended with the words 'Listen to him!' Coming so soon after Caesarea Philippi, they would surely have taken this to mean that they should pay heed to what Jesus had said about his suffering and about the demands of discipleship.

Its importance for Christians

The transfiguration is commemorated by Christians every year on 6 August. Its main importance is connected with the title Son of God. It is also important as a reminder that, for Jesus, suffering and glory went hand in hand.

Summary

You should now know that at the transfiguration Peter, James and John saw Jesus in a vision, and that the symbolism in Mark's account portrays Jesus as the Son of God and the fulfilment of the Old Testament, and confirms Jesus' understanding of his Messiahship.

Study tip

You might be asked in an exam to explain the meaning of the transfiguration. Make sure that you learn and understand the event and its symbolism.

Jesus' ministry – summary

For the examination, you should now be able to:

✓ understand the political and religious background to Jesus' ministry

✓ have a clear overview of the contents of Mark's Gospel

✓ give accounts of the following events:

   – Jesus' baptism and temptation (Mark 1:9–13)

   – Caesarea Philippi (Mark 8:27–33)

   – Jesus' transfiguration (Mark 9:2–8)

✓ understand their significance for Jesus, for his disciples and for Christians.

Sample answer

1 Write an answer to the following exam question:

   Explain how Mark presents Caesarea Philippi as a 'watershed' event in the ministry of Jesus.   *(6 marks)*

2 a Read the sample answer below:

> The conversation at Caesarea Philippi is recorded about half way through Mark's Gospel. Until that point Jesus had spent much of his time teaching the crowds who gathered to hear him. For instance, he taught them about the Kingdom of God, using parables to help them understand. He had also performed a lot of healings and some nature miracles. People saw his authority and were impressed by it. There was some hostility from the religious leaders, but he seemed to be popular with many people. It was near Caesarea Philippi that Peter declared Jesus to be the Messiah. Jesus immediately swore the disciples to secrecy and then went on to teach them about his future rejection, suffering and death, though that would not be the end. Peter found this hard to accept. From that point on, Jesus kept reminding the Twelve of his fate. The Passion predictions all come after Caesarea Philippi. He also concentrated his teaching much more on the Twelve, trying to prepare them for his death. There was less public teaching and fewer miracles. With Caesarea Philippi, the atmosphere of Mark's Gospel changes.

b With a partner, discuss the sample answer. Time for answering questions is limited, so do you think that this answer is relevant and detailed enough to be awarded a good mark? Do you think that, given the time restraints, the candidate has included sufficient details to answer the question fully?

c What mark would you give this answer out of 6? Look at the mark scheme in the Introduction on page 7 (AO1). What are the reasons for the mark you have given?

Practice questions

YOU ARE MY SON, WHOM I LOVE; WITH YOU I AM WELL PLEASED.

THIS IS MY SON, WHOM I LOVE. LISTEN TO HIM!

Mark 1:11 and 9:7

1   **(a)**   Describe the baptism of Jesus.   *(3 marks)*

       (b)   How was the baptism a turning point in the life of Jesus?   *(2 marks)*

2   Outline the temptation of Jesus.   *(2 marks)*

3   Which two Old Testament figures appeared alongside Jesus at the transfiguration?   *(2 marks)*

> **Study tip**   Remember that when you are asked to describe an event, you just retell what happened without any explanation. When asked to explain, you should not retell the story, but should pick out the important bits to help you answer the question.

4   Explain the importance of the transfiguration for Peter, James and John.   *(4 marks)*

> **Study tip**   Remember to only use material from Mark's Gospel in your answers. Do not include any parts of the accounts given by Matthew and Luke. If you do, you will penalise yourself by wasting time.

3.1 The entry into Jerusalem

◼ Jesus' final week in Jerusalem

Jesus came with his disciples to Jerusalem to celebrate Passover. Pilgrims came for Passover from all parts of the Roman Empire. Each year it was a time of both great anticipation and great tension as Jews, resenting the Roman presence, wondered if this would be the year the Messiah would come to bring in the Kingdom of God. Pilate and his soldiers would have been watching carefully for any signs of trouble.

Jesus and his disciples came from Jericho, together with other pilgrims, travelling together for safety on a road that was known for muggings. The story of Jesus' entry into the city marks the start of the final section of Mark's Gospel.

Objectives

Know the story of Jesus' entry into Jerusalem.

Understand the meaning behind the story.

◼ The entry into Jerusalem (11:1–11)

> **Beliefs and teachings**
>
> As they approached Jerusalem and came to Bethphage and Bethany at the Mount of Olives, Jesus sent two of his disciples, saying to them, 'Go to the village ahead of you, and just as you enter it, you will find a colt tied there, which no one has ever ridden. Untie it and bring it here. If anyone asks you, "Why are you doing this?" say, "The Lord needs it and will send it back here shortly." '
>
> They went and found a colt outside in the street, tied at a doorway. As they untied it, some people standing there asked, 'What are you doing, untying that colt?' They answered as Jesus had told them to, and the people let them go. When they brought the colt to Jesus and threw their cloaks over it, he sat on it. Many people spread their cloaks on the road, while others spread branches they had cut in the fields. Those who went ahead and those who followed shouted,
>
> 'Hosanna!'
> 'Blessed is he who comes in the name of the Lord!'
> 'Blessed is the coming kingdom of our father David!'
> 'Hosanna in the highest heaven!'
>
> Jesus entered Jerusalem and went into the temple courts. He looked around at everything, but since it was already late, he went out to Bethany with the Twelve.
>
> *Mark* 11:1–11

This story begins with Jesus sending two disciples to fetch a colt (a young donkey). The detail in this suggests that Mark was told about it by an eyewitness. When the two disciples came back with the colt, they put cloaks on it. As Jesus rode the colt into the city, people carpeted the road with branches and shouted, 'Hosanna! Blessed is he who

A *Jesus' entry into Jerusalem*

B *The Russian Orthodox church is situated on the Mount of Olives*

C *Palm crosses help Christians to remember Jesus' entry into Jerusalem*

comes in the name of the Lord! Blessed is the coming kingdom of our father David!' The impression given by Mark is that it was a celebration involving many people, although those who acclaimed Jesus as Messiah may have been a small group consisting of his disciples and those pilgrims who had travelled with him from Jericho. The vast majority of pilgrims would not have arrived so early in the week, and a large-scale gathering would have alerted the authorities to Jesus' arrival.

■ The significance of this story

This story has great significance. It was customary to enter Jerusalem on foot – only kings rode into the city as a sign of triumph after victories of conquest or authority. According to Mark, Jesus was making a statement by entering Jerusalem riding as a king, but on a colt, to show his humility. The choice of a colt would have been seen as fulfilling the prophecy of Zechariah (see the Beliefs and teachings box). The Messianic Secret was being revealed: Jesus **was** the Messiah, but he came in humility and peace. The reference to the carpet of branches acknowledged his authority. The word 'Hosanna' means 'Save us'. Together with the words about the kingdom of David, it suggests that those with Jesus were hoping that he would free them. Many thought the Messiah would be descended from King David. The other words shouted by the crowd were part of a psalm that was chanted by all pilgrims as they approached Jerusalem.

> **Beliefs and teachings**
>
> Rejoice greatly; O Daughter of Zion!
> Shout, daughter of Jerusalem!
> See, your king comes to you,
> righteous and having salvation,
> gentle and riding on a donkey,
> on a colt, the foal of a donkey.
>
> *Zechariah 9:9*

> **Beliefs and teachings**
>
> O Lord, save us;
> O Lord, grant us success.
> Blessed is he who comes in the name of the Lord.
>
> *Psalm 118:25–26*

Research activity

Palm Sunday

Each year, Christians celebrate Jesus' entry into Jerusalem on Palm Sunday. What happens in many Christian churches and communities on Palm Sunday? Why do you think it is an important day for Christians?

Activities

1. Read Mark 11:1–3. What instructions did Jesus give his two disciples?
2. Christians often refer to this event as 'The triumphal entry'. Why do you think they use this title?
3. How did Jesus' understanding of his role as Messiah differ from the expectations of those who entered Jerusalem with him?

> **Study tip**
>
> Make sure you know both the story of Jesus' entry into Jerusalem, and its significance.

> **Summary**
>
> You should now know the story of Jesus' entry into Jerusalem and understand that by riding on a colt Jesus presented himself as a peaceful Messiah.

3.2 The anointing and arrangements for betrayal

The Sanhedrin's dilemma (Mark 14:1–2)

Beliefs and teachings

Now the Passover and the Feast of Unleavened Bread were only two days away, and the chief priests and the teachers of the law were looking for some sly way to arrest Jesus and kill him. 'But not during the Feast,' they said, 'or the people may riot.'

Mark 14:1–2

According to Mark, the days after Jesus' entry into Jerusalem were largely spent in the Temple, teaching and debating with the religious authorities. Jesus' protest in the Temple was a direct challenge to the Sanhedrin's authority, so they became determined to destroy him. They understood that Jesus' popularity meant an open arrest could have sparked off riots, so they looked for some way to arrest him quietly.

The anointing at Bethany (Mark 14:3–9)

∞ links

Read the set text Mark 14:3–9 in your Bible before reading the analysis of this story.

After the protest in the Temple, Mark relates the story of Jesus' anointing by a woman. The woman's sudden appearance at the dinner party and her actions would have shocked the men who were with Jesus. It was customary to anoint guests at a meal, but it was unthinkable for a woman to do it, and to use such an expensive oil. The sharp criticisms must have humiliated the woman. Jesus' reply was important for three reasons:

- He understood the woman's motivation and praised her generosity.
- He saw her as performing burial preparation rites, anticipating his death.
- He said her action would always be remembered, wherever his story was told.

In Old Testament times, kings were anointed as a sign that they had been chosen by God and had a unique relationship with him. The word 'Messiah' means 'anointed one'.

Arrangements for betrayal (Mark 14:10–11)

The Sanhedrin had been powerless to get rid of Jesus, but now their chance came. The nature of the arrangements is not clear, but Judas probably offered to tell them where Jesus could be arrested privately, avoiding a public outcry. Mark conveys horror at Judas' actions. Each time he refers to the betrayal, the phrase 'one of the Twelve' is used, emphasising that one of Jesus' chosen companions was the traitor.

Objectives

Know the story of the anointing at Bethany and to understand its significance.

Understand possible reasons for Judas' decision to betray Jesus.

∞ links

To find out about: the disputes with the authorities, see pages 96–101; the Sanhedrin, see pages 32–33; the Temple, see pages 34–35.

A *Judas betraying Jesus to the chief priests*

Beliefs and teachings

Then Judas Iscariot, one of the Twelve, went to the chief priests to betray Jesus to them. They were delighted to hear this and promised to give him some money. So he watched for an opportunity to hand him over.

Mark 14:10–11

Who was Judas?

Apart from the betrayal, nothing else is known for certain about Judas. The name Iscariot is not a surname, and some scholars think it means 'man of Kerioth', a town in Judaea. Others think he was a Zealot, linking Iscariot with the Latin *sicarii* (daggermen) who stabbed their chosen victims in crowded places. It is known that at least one other member of the Twelve was a Zealot.

Why did Judas betray Jesus?

Until this point, Judas had presumably followed Jesus with the same commitment as the rest of the Twelve. Some people think his motive in betraying Jesus was greed, as he was promised a fee. Others think he had expected Jesus to lead a rebellion against the Romans. If so, Jesus' statement on taxes earlier in the week, making it clear that the people should obey Roman laws, would have made him unhappy. The reference to 'anointing for burial' made it clear that Jesus was not going to start an uprising. Judas was perhaps so disillusioned that he turned traitor. It is also possible that Judas wanted to force Jesus to act to save himself – and that this action would lead to the desired uprising.

Nobody can know Judas' motives for sure. The New Testament writers, including Mark, were more concerned to see the events leading up to and including Jesus' death as part of God's plan. Judas' decision, though freely chosen, helped in fulfilling that plan.

links

To read about the Zealots, see pages 32–33.

links

For the full story of Jesus' statement on taxes, read Mark 12:13–17 and 5:4.

Discussion activity

1 Divide into four groups. Each group should discuss one of the following questions, and then report back, then open the discussion up to everyone.

a Why do you think the Sanhedrin would have been anxious to prevent trouble among the crowds during Passover week?

b What do Jesus' words about the beautiful nature of the woman's action suggest about his character?

c How does the anointing link Jesus' Messiahship with suffering?

d Why do you think Judas betrayed Jesus: greed, disillusionment or the belief that Jesus needed to stand up to the Romans using force?

Research activity

Judas Iscariot

1 a Find out about Judas by reading Mark 3:13–19; 14:17–20, 43–45. Then read the two different accounts of his death in Matthew 27:3–5 and Acts 1:18.

b How do these stories reflect early Christian views on Judas?

c Taking into account your research and the information contained in the pages of this book, what are your own views about Judas?

Extension activity

Using a library or a search engine, find and read the 19th-century poem *Saint Brandan* by Matthew Arnold. This poem gives a different perspective on Judas. Does reading it change your attitude to Judas?

Study tip

The three texts studied on these pages (Mark 14:1–2, 3–9 and 10–11) are all set texts, so make sure you know and understand them.

Summary

You should now understand why the religious authorities wished to be rid of Jesus; how Jesus' anointing at Bethany pointed to his Messianic identity and to his imminent death; and know the story of Judas' offer to betray Jesus.

3.3 The Last Supper

■ Introduction

Passover is a very important Jewish festival. In the 1st century it was celebrated in Jerusalem, as sacrifices could only be offered in the Temple. The Passover meal included sacrificed lamb, unleavened bread and wine. The Jews reclined (a symbol of freedom) as they ate and retold the story of how God rescued the Israelites from Egypt.

■ Preparations for the Passover (14:12–16)

∞ links

Read this set text in Mark 14:12–16, about the preparations for the Passover meal in Jesus' last week.

Jesus had arranged for the Passover meal to be in an upper room. The instructions Jesus gave to the two disciples who prepared everything seem strange: they had to follow a man carrying a water jar (a rare sight) and then were told exactly what to say to the householder. Perhaps, in front of the whole group, including Judas, Jesus did not want to say openly where it was to be held.

■ The Last Supper (14:17–25)

Prediction of betrayal

> **Beliefs and teachings**
>
> When evening came, Jesus arrived with the Twelve. While they were reclining at the table eating, he said, 'Truly I tell you, one of you will betray me – one who is eating with me.'
>
> They were saddened, and one by one they said to him, 'Surely not I?'
>
> 'It is one of the Twelve,' he replied, 'one who dips bread into the bowl with me. The Son of Man will go just as it is written about him. But woe to that man who betrays the Son of Man! It would be better for him if he had not been born.'
>
> *Mark* 14:17–21

Jesus and the Twelve arrived at the upper room in the evening, and Jesus warned that one of them was about to betray him. He did not indicate who it was, but he emphasised the fact that it was one of those eating with him. Sharing food was a sign of intimate friendship, so Jesus' words highlighted the awfulness of the act of betrayal. It was no wonder that the disciples were distressed, each seeking reassurance that it was not him. Referring to himself as the Son of Man, Jesus stated that his death was part of God's purpose for him. Yet, at the same time the traitor was responsible for his action: it would have been better had he never been born.

Objectives

Study Mark's account of the Last Supper.

Understand its meaning for Jesus, his disciples and Christians.

A *A seder dish – the special plate used at Passover*

> **Beliefs and teachings**
>
> While they were eating, Jesus took bread, gave thanks and broke it, and gave it to his disciples, saying, 'Take it; this is my body.' Then he took the cup, gave thanks and offered it to them, and they all drank from it. 'This is my blood of the covenant, which is poured out for many,' he said to them. 'I tell you the truth. I will not drink again of the fruit of the vine until that day when I drink it anew in the kingdom of God.'
>
> *Mark* 14:22–25

The meaning of the Last Supper for Jesus and his disciples

Why did Jesus refer to the traitor? Maybe he was hoping Judas would have second thoughts. Jesus accepted God's purpose for him to die, but Judas did not have to be the means of achieving it.

The words about the bread and wine gave the Passover meal a new meaning. In sharing the bread and wine, the disciples were united with one another and with Jesus through his death. Although Mark did not record Jesus' command to repeat this meal, the early Christian community did repeat it on a regular basis right from the start.

Jesus finally stated that he would not drink wine again until he did so in the Kingdom of God. The Messianic Banquet was a Jewish symbol for the Kingdom of God, representing the joy that would be part of the new age. Jesus was perhaps implying that the Kingdom of God would arrive with his death.

B   *A stained glass window depicting the Last Supper*

Activities

1   Why do you think Passover would have been both a happy and a sad time for the Jews of Jesus' day? If you are not sure, read again pages 30–31.

2   Why do you think Jesus might not have wanted Judas to know where they would be celebrating Passover?

3   Why was the image of a feast an appropriate symbol for the Kingdom of God?

Discussion activity

Although he knew that Judas was about to betray him, Jesus included him in the Last Supper, giving him the bread and the wine. Why do you think he did this? If you had been Jesus, would you have been able to do this? You need to remember that eating together was a symbol of intimate friendship. Think how you feel when someone close to you lets you down or hurts you.

The meaning of the Last Supper for Christians

Many Christians celebrate the Last Supper in the service of Holy Communion. There are a number of different names for this service, and there are also many interpretations of the words: 'This is my body' and 'This is my blood', but all Christians believe that the bread and wine are linked to Jesus' crucifixion. At Holy Communion, they believe that they are re-enacting or remembering Jesus' sacrificial death and sharing in his risen life. They are united with him and with one another, and they receive spiritual strength to help them be faithful disciples in their everyday lives.

C   *A priest celebrating Holy Communion*

Study tip

When writing an account of what Jesus said and did in connection with the bread and wine, make sure that you use the phrasing in Mark's Gospel and not that used at Holy Communion services.

Summary

You should now be able to give an account of the Last Supper and to understand its meaning for Jesus, his disciples and Christians.

3.4 Jesus in Gethsemane

■ Jesus' time of prayer (Mark 14:32–42)

Gethsemane (which means 'oil press') was probably an olive orchard. It is on the slopes of the Mount of Olives, overlooking Jerusalem. By the time Jesus and his disciples arrived at Gethsemane, Judas was no longer with them. Telling the others to sit and wait, Jesus took Peter, James and John with him, asking them to stay awake. He desperately needed their support, as he was in mental torment.

∞ links

Mark 14:26–31 is a set text linking the Last Supper to Gethsemane. For more information on this, and to read the text, see pages 122–123.

In his distress, he begged God to take away the cup, a metaphor for suffering and death, from him. Mark gave the actual Aramaic word Jesus used to address God: 'Abba'. Jesus was afraid, yet at the same time, he said he would go ahead with God's will. On returning to the three, he discovered that they had fallen asleep and he reproached Peter. Though mentally prepared to remain awake, Peter and the other two had given in to physical weakness. Twice more Jesus prayed and again found them asleep. As he prayed, he could probably see Judas and the Levite guards leaving the city, crossing the Kidron valley and climbing up the Mount of Olives, and so he now told his disciples to wake up as his betrayer had arrived.

A *This church is thought to be on the site where Jesus prayed*

The importance of this event to Christians

Many Christians feel that they can relate to Jesus in this story. He knew what awaited him and was terrified. Like most people, he did not want to die, especially not by the long and painful method of crucifixion. Christians are also inspired by his obedience to God and his humble trust: the word he used for God, *Abba*, was that used to a father by a trusting child. For those 1st-century Christians facing persecution and to any Christian afraid of the future, this story might be a source of encouragement. It showed that it was not wrong to be afraid; what mattered was trust in, and obedience to, God.

Many Christians can also relate to Peter, James and John. They wanted to stay awake, but could not. Despite their declared readiness to share in Jesus' suffering, they could not live up to their promises. Nevertheless, however deeply Jesus needed their support and felt let down by them, he understood. This might have inspired Mark's readers not to despair if their faith had failed them in the crisis of persecution.

B *In Gethsemane Jesus trusted God as a child trusts its father*

Activities

1. Why do you think many people (both Christian and non-Christian) find Judas' action on this occasion so terrible?
2. Why do you think Jesus was not arrested earlier in the week when he was teaching in the Temple? If you are unsure, read again pages 52–53.
3. Why was Jesus able to remain calm?
4. Why did the disciples panic?

■ Jesus' arrest (Mark 14:43–52)

∞ links

Read the set text Mark 14:43–52 before reading the analysis of the story below.

Judas arrived and kissed Jesus. This was the usual way a disciple greeted his rabbi, but on this occasion it was the pre-arranged form of identification. Jesus was arrested by the armed Levites and a scuffle broke out. Jesus offered no resistance, simply pointing out that the Levites, unarmed, could have arrested him at any point earlier in the week when he was teaching in the Temple. He saw his arrest, however, as fulfilling the Old Testament. At that point his disciples fled, abandoning him to his fate. The young man who was seized by his undergarment and also ran off into the night, naked, is thought to have been John Mark.

The reactions of Jesus and his disciples were very different. Jesus had spent time in prayer and, when the moment of arrest came, accepted it calmly as God's will. The disciples, however, had slept and were unprepared. They panicked and, going against all they had said a few hours before, ran for their lives.

C *The kiss of betrayal*

Study tip

Remember these stories when you study Chapters 4 (The person of Jesus) and 6 (Discipleship). When writing, for instance, about the disciples, you can refer to material from any part of Mark's Gospel to make your points.

Summary

You should now know the stories of Jesus' prayer in Gethsemane and his arrest, understanding what Christians might learn from them about the person of Jesus and about the twelve disciples.

Introduction

Rules governing Sanhedrin trials

There were strict rules governing Jewish Council (Sanhedrin) trials where the death penalty was involved:

- A trial should not be held at night or on the eve of a Jewish feast day.
- A final verdict must not be given until a day had passed, to encourage the court to show mercy.
- The trial itself should be held in the Hall of Hewn Stone.
- The trial should begin with reasons for finding the accused person innocent.
- Evidence was only valid if given by two witnesses whose testimony agreed.
- The high priest, who presided over the trial, should not ask direct questions.
- A conviction for blasphemy should only be given where God's personal name (Exodus 3:14) was used.
- The Jewish penalty for blasphemy was stoning to death. Because of the Roman occupation, however, the Sanhedrin could not carry out the death sentence. There had to be a Roman trial. If the accused was again found guilty then the Roman method of execution must be used: crucifixion.

Why were the rules broken in Jesus' trial?

Mark's account of Jesus' trial shows that these rules were broken. Some scholars think that the account of the incident has deliberately emphasised that the Jews were responsible for Jesus' death. This would make sense in a time of Roman persecution and Christians in 1st-century Rome would not have wanted to anger the authorities by blaming them for Jesus' death. However, as the Sanhedrin would normally have kept to the rules for trials, it may be that the Jews were so desperate to be rid of Jesus without trouble that they made the most of their opportunity, regardless of the rules. Providing nothing went wrong with the Roman trial, Jesus would then have been on the way to his death before the general public was aware of what was happening.

> **Objectives**
>
> Study Jesus' trial before the Sanhedrin (Jewish Council) and understand why it did not follow the accepted rules for such trials.
>
> Consider reasons why Jesus was found guilty.

A *Jesus before the high priest Caiaphas*

Activity

1. Create a table with two columns. Head the first column: 'Rules for Jewish trials'. List in that column the rules that governed Sanhedrin trials. Head the second column: 'The trial of Jesus by the Sanhedrin'. Under this column, list the features of that trial that correspond to, or conflict with, the rules you have put in the first column.

■ Jesus' trial before the Sanhedrin (Mark 14:53–65)

⬭ links

Study carefully the set text Mark 14:53–65 before reading this analysis of the trial.

All the evidence given against Jesus at his trial at the high priest's house conflicted. According to some witnesses, Jesus had said that he would destroy the Temple and in three days build another, not man-made. The Jews believed that in the new age, God or the Messiah would rebuild the Temple. So this statement would have been seen as a false Messianic claim and as deeply insulting to Jews. The words 'three days' probably just meant a short time, but Mark and his readers would have related it to Jesus' Resurrection, three days after his death. The high priest tried in vain to get Jesus to answer the charges. Finally in frustration, he asked a direct question.

Both the high priest and Jesus avoided direct reference to God by name, as this would be blasphemy, but Jesus' reply was clear. He stated that he was both Messiah and Son of God. Yet still he called himself the Son of Man. He said that he would be given supreme authority by God and would judge humanity when this world came to an end. The high priest interpreted his reply as blasphemous. Perhaps he took Jesus' words 'I am' to be the first part of God's name as revealed to Moses. Or it may be that to find Jesus' guilty, he accepted a looser definition of blasphemy. He tore his coat, the symbolic action marking the end of a trial, signifying his grief and horror at the blasphemy, and all those present agreed that Jesus deserved to die. Those guarding Jesus for the rest of the night beat him, mocking him as a false prophet.

> **Beliefs and teachings**
>
> Again the high priest asked him, 'Are you the Christ, the Son of the Blessed One?' 'I am,' said Jesus. 'And you will see the Son of Man sitting at the right hand of the Mighty One and coming on the clouds of heaven.'
>
> *Mark 14:61–62*

> **Beliefs and teachings**
>
> God said to Moses, 'I AM WHO I AM.'
>
> *Exodus 3:14*

⬭ links

Read pages 96–97 and 104–105 for more about why the Jewish religious authorities believed Jesus was leading people astray.

> **Activity**
>
> 2 Answer the following questions from memory. Then use both Mark 14:53–65 and this book to check your answers.
>
> a What evidence was given against Jesus?
>
> b What was Jesus' response when the high priest asked him to reply to the accusations?
>
> c What question did the high priest finally ask?
>
> d What was Jesus' answer?
>
> e What titles did Jesus accept and use of himself?
>
> f What did the high priest then do and say?
>
> g How did the guards show their contempt for Jesus?

> **Study tip**
>
> You must be able to give an accurate account of this trial if asked to do so in an examination. Make sure that you do not confuse it with the trial before Pilate (which is covered on pages 60–61).

> **Discussion activity** 👥
>
> The Sanhedrin believed that Jesus was leading the Jewish people astray. This was because Jesus broke the oral tradition that had been developed by the scribes and was intended to help people keep the Torah. He also mixed with immoral people, which scandalised them and challenged their authority. Do you think this justified the Sanhedrin breaking the rules of trials on this occasion? Can you think of any occasion, either in your life or more generally, when breaking rules was justified? Can you think of any situation when you might be prepared to 'bend' rules that you would normally follow?

> **Summary**
>
> You should now be able to give a detailed and accurate account of Jesus' trial before the Sanhedrin, showing understanding of how and why Jewish rules were broken. You should know that Jesus was convicted of blasphemy, and why.

3.6 Jesus' trial before Pilate

Introduction

Pilate was Prefect (his official title) of Judaea from 26–36 CE. In the 1st century he was assessed as a cruel, stubborn and inflexible man. He was eventually dismissed from his position because of all the complaints made against him. Some scholars think that this conflicts with Mark's account of Jesus' trial, in which Pilate gave in to the will of the crowd after doing his best to have Jesus released. They suggest that this was part of Mark's emphasis on the Jews' responsibility for Jesus' death. Pilate's action may, however, have been motivated by the complaints already made against him. He must have been aware of the need to 'tread carefully', especially at Passover time. Had he released Jesus, malicious reports might have been made to the emperor that Pilate had set free a revolutionary.

The trial before Pilate (Mark 15: 1–20)

∞ links

Read the set text Mark 15:1–20 before going on to read the analysis of this story below.

The trial would have taken place very early on the Friday of Jesus' last week, and can be divided up into three sections: the Sanhedrin bringing Jesus to Pilate after a quick meeting to prepare the case; the actual trial; and the mockery by the Roman soldiers. The location would have been either the Tower of Antonia adjacent to the Temple or Herod's palace.

Preparation of the case against Jesus

The short morning meeting of the Sanhedrin was probably to prepare the case against Jesus. He had been convicted of blasphemy, but this was a Jewish religious offence and Pilate would not have been interested in it. The charge needed to be political to gain the attention of the prefect. Since Jesus had said he was the Messiah, it was not difficult to alter the case. The Romans understood the idea of a Messiah as referring to a political figure, a king. Claiming to be a king was treason, for which the Roman penalty was crucifixion.

Jesus' trial

When asked if he was the king of the Jews, Jesus gave an ambiguous response. He was perhaps indicating that he was their king in a religious but not a political sense. He refused to say anything more, which amazed Pilate – with his vast experience of Jewish revolutionaries, the prefect could see that there was no real case against Jesus.

It is possible that Pilate decided to release a prisoner at the Passover to encourage peace in Jerusalem at this time of tension. A crowd had arrived to make their request. Pilate saw this as a way of getting Jesus released without antagonising the Sanhedrin, but his plan

A *A coin minted by Pilate during the ministry of Jesus*

Beliefs and teachings

'Are you the king of the Jews?' asked Pilate.

'You have said so,' Jesus replied.

The chief priests accused him of many things. So again Pilate asked him, 'Aren't you going to answer? See how many things they are accusing you of.'

But Jesus still made no reply, and Pilate was amazed.

Mark 15:2–5

B *Jesus before Pilate*

Study tip

When writing an account of Jesus' trial before Pilate, make sure that you do not include material from other gospels or details that you might have seen in films. You must only include material from Mark's Gospel in the exam.

backfired. The crowd were probably supporters of Barabbas, who had been involved in an uprising. If so, it was not difficult for the Jewish authorities to whip them up into near hysteria in their support of Barabbas. Pilate's repeated question as to what he should do with Jesus might have been attempts to get Jesus freed, or simply his way of annoying the Jews, whom he despised. Whatever the reason, Pilate could see that the situation could get out of control, and so he granted their request and released Barabbas. Jesus was given the terrible whipping that usually preceded crucifixion and was then handed over to the soldiers for crucifixion.

The mocking of Jesus

The charge of being 'king of the Jews' formed the basis for the soldiers' treatment of Jesus. The soldiers dressed him in a cloak of imperial purple and gave him a crown of thorns, mimicking the emperor's laurel wreath crown. 'Hail, king of the Jews!' was a parody of 'Hail, Caesar!' and they paid him mock homage. They also hit him with a cane and spat on him.

C *Jesus was dressed in a purple cloak and crown of thorns*

⚭links

Use the following link to help with the research activity: **www.bible-history.com**.

⚭links

Texts for the discussion: the arrest, Mark 14:43–52; the trial before the Sanhedrin, Mark 14:53–65; the trial before Pilate 15:1–20.

Research activity

Pontius Pilate

Divide into groups of three. Look up the website listed in the Links opposite. Type 'Pilate' into 'Search' and then click on 'The Pilate Inscription'. Prepare a presentation for the rest of the class on one of the following paragraphs on the webpage: 'Who was Pontius Pilate?', 'The Roman Procurator', or 'Pontius Pilate and the Jews'. You should cover all three paragraphs between you. If you cannot access this site, search for other websites on Pilate to complete this task.

Discussion activity

Read again Mark's account of the arrangements for betrayal, the arrest and the trials before the Sanhedrin and Pilate, along with the relevant pages in this book. Discuss in small groups the following question: Who was most responsible for the death of Jesus: the Sanhedrin, Pilate, the crowd at the Roman trial, Judas or Jesus himself?

Summary

You should now understand that Pilate knew the charges against Jesus were weak, but he sentenced Jesus to death for claiming to be king of the Jews, and that responsibility for Jesus' crucifixion is complicated, with various people and groups involved.

3.7 The crucifixion and burial (1)

Introduction

Crucifixion was an inhumane and humiliating form of killing, intended to deter others from offending. It was the standard punishment for slaves, rebels and those who committed serious crimes. (Roman citizens were not crucified but beheaded.) After being beaten, the victim carried the crossbeam to the place of execution, always a very public place. There he was roped or nailed to the cross through the wrists and ankles. The details of the crime were put on the cross, again as a deterrent to passers-by. Death was usually slow and agonising. According to Jewish law, a body should not remain hanging overnight, so sometimes a request was granted for the body to be taken down before sunset. If necessary the soldiers would take action to hasten death. Relatives or friends could only take the body for burial, however, if permission had been given by the Roman governor.

The crucifixion of Jesus (Mark 15:21–41)

links

Read the set text Mark 15:21–41 before moving on; also read Psalm 22, which many believed foretold Jesus' crucifixion.

Mark must have received his information about the crucifixion from someone present, possibly the women. However, Old Testament texts, particularly Psalm 22, may have affected the way he described it. Both Mark and 1st-century Christians would have believed that Jesus' death was foretold in the Old Testament.

Mark's account falls into three parts: the process of crucifixion; the taunts of those who saw Jesus; and the final moments leading up to and following on from his death.

The process of crucifixion

Jesus had experienced the emotional trauma of betrayal, desertion and denial by his friends and endured the stress of two trials. He was twice beaten, and the floggings given by the Roman soldiers were so severe that victims sometimes died. It is not surprising, therefore, that he found the heavy weight of the crossbeam too much. The soldiers picked on a passer-by, Simon, from Cyrene in North Africa, and made him carry it to the place of crucifixion, Golgotha (which means 'The Place of the Skull'). Simon had probably come to Jerusalem as a Passover pilgrim.

A *The Via Dolorosa in Jerusalem – the road along which Jesus was taken to his crucifixion*

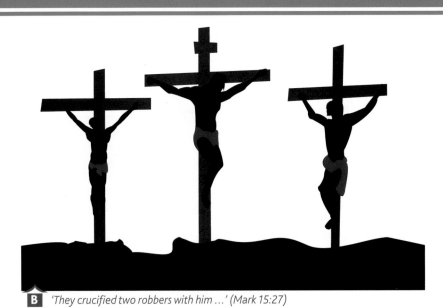

B *'They crucified two robbers with him ...' (Mark 15:27)*

The custom of drugged drink being offered as an act of kindness, probably by Jewish women, was mentioned in early Jewish writings. Jesus refused it, presumably to show that he willingly accepted his suffering. Soldiers had to remain on guard throughout the execution, to prevent any attempt at rescue, and the victims' possessions became their property. The crucifixion was under way by 9am. Two others, probably associates of Barabbas, were crucified alongside Jesus. The inscription on Jesus' cross, 'The King of the Jews', pointed to his crime as political.

The taunts

Passers-by referred in mockery to the statement brought as evidence against Jesus in the Jewish trial, that he would destroy the temple and rebuild it in three days. Jewish religious leaders also taunted him, laughing at the contrast between his ability to perform miracles in the past and his helplessness on the cross. Even those suffering the same fate insulted him. Jesus was completely alone, utterly isolated.

C *The Church of the Holy Sepulchre, built over the site of Golgotha and place of Jesus' burial*

Activities

1 Why do you think Roman citizens were not crucified?
2 Why did the Romans use crucifixion as the form of execution for certain criminals?
3 Why was Simon of Cyrene made to carry Jesus' cross?
4 Why must Jesus have felt so alone?

Summary

You should now know Mark's account of the crucifixion and understand the way in which he emphasises the humanity of Jesus.

Study tip

In reading Mark's account of the crucifixion, bear in mind that he was writing for Christians facing hostility and persecution. In what ways does his account relate to their situation?

The death of Jesus (Mark 15:34–41)

∞ links

Read the account of Jesus' crucifixion in Mark 15: 21–41, especially verse 34 onwards, before moving on.

The climax of the crucifixion is reached with Jesus' final words and death, the tearing of the Temple curtain, the centurion's statement and the reference to the presence of the women. As with much of Mark's Gospel, the account is full of symbolic meaning. It must have had deep significance for those Christians whose faith was being severely tested in 1st-century Rome.

> **Beliefs and teachings**
>
> And at three in the afternoon Jesus cried out in a loud voice, 'Eloi, Eloi, lema sabachthani?' (which means 'My God, my God, why have you forsaken me?').
>
> When some of those standing near heard this, they said, 'Listen, he's calling Elijah.'
>
> Someone ran, filled a sponge with wine vinegar, put it on a staff, and offered it to Jesus to drink. 'Now leave him alone. Let's see if Elijah comes to take him down,' he said.
>
> With a loud cry, Jesus breathed his last.
>
> The curtain of the temple was torn in two from top to bottom. And when the centurion, who stood there in front of Jesus, saw how he died, he said, 'Surely this man was the Son of God!'
>
> Some women were watching from a distance. Among them were Mary Magdalene, Mary the mother of James the younger and of Joseph, and Salome. In Galilee these women had followed him and cared for his needs. Many other women who had come up with him to Jerusalem were also there.
>
> *Mark* 15:34–41

Jesus' final hours and death

Mark recorded that from midday there was darkness for three hours over Israel. There might have been storm clouds caused either by rain or a desert wind, but many scholars think this was intended to be taken symbolically as a sign of the terrible sin that had been committed in crucifying Jesus. Judgement was being passed on Israel for having rejected the Messiah. By 3pm Jesus was near death and cried out in anguish. The Aramaic words he used, which were a quotation from Psalm 22, meaning 'My God, my God, why have you forsaken me?', were remembered and passed on. Though loud, what Jesus said may have been indistinct, as some of those watching thought that he was calling Elijah. The Jews believed that Elijah would return to help good people in times of trouble. So they tried to prolong Jesus' life by offering him some of their cheap wine, to see if Jesus' appeal was answered. Jesus, however, gave one last shout and died.

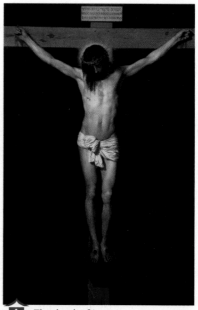

A *The death of Jesus*

B   *'At the sixth hour darkness came over the whole land until the ninth hour.'*

The tearing of the Temple curtain

Many scholars think that Mark included the tearing of the Temple curtain because of its symbolic meaning. The curtain separated off the Holy of Holies, the central part of the Temple where only God was present. Mark may be suggesting that Jesus' death tore down the barrier of sin that cut humanity off from God.

The centurion's statement

The centurion was the Roman officer responsible for overseeing the crucifixion of Jesus and the two other men. He was so impressed by the manner of Jesus' death that he stated, 'Surely this man was the Son of God!' He probably meant that Jesus was in some way a divine or special man. For Mark, however, his words meant far more. They were a declaration of the real truth about Jesus. This would have been highly significant for Christians in 1st-century Rome. The Jewish people had mostly rejected Jesus; it was the centurion, a Gentile like most of those who recognised and declared his true identity, who spoke these words. This was a clear statement that the good news was for everyone.

The women

The disciples were nowhere to be seen. It was left to the women, who had looked after Jesus throughout his ministry, to witness his crucifixion. These final verses of the crucifixion story must have been very important for 1st-century Christian women, who were often looked down on for their gender.

links

For information on the location and significance of the Temple curtain, read pages 34–35.

C   *The women witnessed Jesus' crucifixion*

Study tip

When answering exam questions, it is important to take note of exactly what you are asked to do. If you are required to describe something, you should not include comment or explanation.

Activity

1   a   Read the whole of the set text discussed on pages 62–65, Mark 15:21–41. Then, without referring to your Bible or any other books, describe Jesus' crucifixion, from when he set out for Golgotha to Mark's reference to the presence of the women.

   b   Check what you have written to ensure that you have included most of what happened. You do not need to include any explanation of the symbolism.

Summary

You should now know in detail Mark's account of Jesus' crucifixion and understand some of its significance for 1st-century Christians.

■ The meaning of Jesus' death for Christians

⬀links

Re-read the account of Jesus' crucifixion in Mark 15:21–41 before working through the rest of these pages.

Right from the start, Christians thought about the significance of Jesus' death. Early Christian preaching stressed that together with Jesus' Resurrection, it was part of God's plan for saving mankind. Throughout the centuries, Christian thinkers have put forward and continue to suggest many ideas on the significance of the crucifixion, some of which are considered here.

Self-giving love

Christians have interpreted Jesus' last cry, 'My God, my God, why have you forsaken me?' in different ways. Some think that in order to cope with his ordeal Jesus remembered Psalm 22, which starts in despair but ends with trust in God's deliverance. Others think that at his death he took on the sin of humanity and experienced the separation that it created between God and humans. Many Christians believe that this moment shows the full extent of Jesus' self-sacrificial love. He willingly accepted his fate, even though it meant he felt cut off from God, and set an example for people to follow.

The importance for Christians of Jesus' words from the cross

> ❝ Jesus now experiences the most bitter blow which can befall the religious man: the sense of having been abandoned by God. Mark reminds his readers of the horror of Jesus' sufferings … His willingness to 'deny himself and … lose his life' has been tested to the full. Only because he is willing to drain the cup of suffering to the full (Mark 10:38; 14:36) will he be vindicated, and his proclamation as king be turned from a mockery into a reality. ❞
>
> M. Hooker, The Gospel according to St Mark

Discussion activity 👥👥👥

1 Read again through Mark 15:21–34 and the different explanations given for Jesus' final words on page 64. If possible, read also the whole of Psalm 22. In pairs or small groups, discuss which of the suggestions made about Jesus' words makes most sense to you, and why? What does each of those suggestions imply about Jesus' feelings at that moment?

Objectives

Explore the significance of Jesus' death for Christians.

Study Mark's account of Jesus' burial.

⬀links

For more on Jesus' Resurrection, see pages 68–73.

Beliefs and teachings

For he has not despised or disdained the suffering of the afflicted one; he has not hidden his face from him but has listened to his cry for help … They will proclaim his righteousness to a people yet unborn – for he has done it.

Psalms 22:24, 31

A Christians believe that Jesus' death was an act of self-sacrificial love

Atonement

Atonement literally means 'at-one-ment' and refers to reconciliation, or bringing together. Christians believe that human sinfulness built up a barrier to God that humans could not remove. The death of Jesus, who took on all human sin, removed that barrier, enabling people to move closer to God. This explains the reference in Mark's Gospel to Jesus' cry of despair and to the tearing of the Temple curtain. It also links to the reference that Jesus made to his death being a ransom.

Liberation

Some Christians refer to Jesus' death as setting humans free from sin and opening up the possibility of eternal life. Christians who are repressed by corrupt governments may think of Jesus' life and death in this way. It enables them to cope with their difficulties, while at the same time working peacefully for change.

Victory

Jesus' ministry may have appeared to have ended in failure and defeat. But Christians believe that the cross proclaimed him as a victor, like a king who proclaims his victory, because in willingly accepting his suffering, Jesus conquered evil, and in his self-sacrifice, love conquered hate.

Beliefs and teachings

For even the Son of Man did not come to be served, but to serve, and to give his life as a ransom for many.

Mark 10:45

B   *Poor or oppressed Christians may see Jesus' death as liberating them from their difficult circumstances*

Discussion activity 👥👥👥

2   Divide into four groups, each taking a different idea about the meaning of Jesus' death for Christians from the notes here. From what you know so far about Jesus' life and death, discuss why Christians might find the idea you have chosen helpful. Give a summary of your discussion to the rest of the class. You might wish to consider which idea you find most useful, and why.

Study tip

It is very important to know why Jesus' death is important to Christians. You might be asked to write about this in the exam.

■ The burial of Jesus (Mark 15:42–47)

∞ links

Read the set text Mark 15:42–46, before moving on. For more on the emergence of false beliefs, read pages 20–21.

It was important for Mark to record the burial. False beliefs about Jesus were emerging, including the belief that he did not actually die. Mark needed to show that this was untrue. The repeated references to Jesus being dead and the check Pilate made show that his death was a confirmed fact.

It took courage for Joseph to request the body; Pilate could have refused his request. Joseph was a member of the Council (probably meaning the Sanhedrin). So why did he request the body of the man the Sanhedrin had sent to his death? Maybe he had not been present at Jesus' trial. The meeting must have been called quickly and he might have gone home after the Passover meal. He may have been a secret supporter of Jesus or simply a devout Jew, horrified at the idea of the body being left hanging overnight.

Jesus was placed in a burial cave. Such caves cut out of the rock were common in Judaea, and it was normal to seal them with a stone. Because Sabbath was so near, there was no time to anoint the body.

C   *Joseph bought a linen cloth in which to wrap Jesus' body*

Summary

You should now understand the importance of Jesus' death for Christians and know Mark's account of the burial of Jesus.

The empty tomb (Mark 16:1–8)

Beliefs and teachings

When the Sabbath was over, Mary Magdalene, Mary the mother of James, and Salome bought spices so that they might go to anoint Jesus' body. Very early on the first day of the week, just after sunrise, they were on their way to the tomb and they asked each other, 'Who will roll the stone away from the entrance of the tomb?' But when they looked up, they saw that the stone, which was very large, had been rolled away. As they entered the tomb, they saw a young man dressed in a white robe sitting on the right side, and they were alarmed. 'Don't be alarmed,' he said. 'You are looking for Jesus the Nazarene, who was crucified. He has risen! He is not here. See the place where they laid him. But go, tell his disciples and Peter, "He is going ahead of you into Galilee. There you will see him, just as he told you."' Trembling and bewildered, the women went out and fled from the tomb. They said nothing to anyone, because they were afraid.

Mark 16:1–8

This story is full of significance.

The young man in white

The young man in white was understood by Mark to be an angel.

The women

The women had been witnesses to Jesus' death and burial; now they were the first to hear the good news of his **Resurrection**. Jewish women were important only in the home, and were often despised in wider society. (For example, a Jewish woman's evidence in a legal case did not count unless her husband confirmed it.) It is remarkable that Mary and her companions were singled out in this way. The women, who had been faithful right up to this point, were now so terrified by the experience that they too failed, at least for the moment. They fled from the tomb, telling no one about it.

The message for the disciples

The message that the women were told to give the eleven disciples is also full of meaning. They had all failed Jesus but were assured of forgiveness. They were to go to Galilee, where they had first been called to follow Jesus. There, they would see him again and be able to make a fresh start. Peter was singled out for special mention, as he had actually denied Jesus.

Objectives

Study Mark's account of the empty tomb.

Investigate the debate about the ending of Mark's Gospel at 16:8.

A Mark's Gospel ends with the woman running away from the tomb, terrified

Key terms

Resurrection: when Jesus rose from the dead after dying on the cross. One of the key beliefs of Christianity.

∞ links

For Jesus telling the disciples that he would go before them into Galilee after the Resurrection, read page 122.

Activities

1   How does Mark indicate that the young man was an angel? (If you are unsure about this, read again about Jesus' transfiguration on pages 46–47.)

2   Why is it surprising that according to Mark's Gospel women were the first to learn of Jesus' Resurrection?

3   Why was the message for the disciples important?

■ The debate about the end of Mark's Gospel

Although many modern versions of the gospel contain verses 9–20, most scholars agree that they were added in the 2nd century CE, and that Mark's Gospel ended at verse 8 with the words 'because they were afraid'. This verse is so abrupt, especially in Greek, that many think Mark could not have intended it to be the end of his gospel. Moreover, it is claimed, the gospel is meant to be good news. To end at verse 8 would be to end on a note of fear and despair.

Why might Mark have ended at verse 8?

There are several theories as to why Mark might have ended his gospel at verse 8. It could be that he died before he finished the gospel. In that case, perhaps he perished in Nero's persecution. The gospel would have been written in columns on parchment scrolls. It might be that what was written after verse 8 was in a new column on the outside of the scroll and was destroyed through continual use. If so, this must have occurred very early before any copying. It is surprising that if this happened, nobody wrote it out again.

B *A parchment scroll like the ones Mark would have used*

Some, however, believe that Mark intended to end his gospel at verse 8. Mark's Greek was not good, so the abruptness is less surprising than it might seem. Some scholars claim that the amazement and fear felt by the women is highly appropriate and the reader is left to reflect on the story of Jesus' life and death, knowing of the belief in the Resurrection and experiencing the continuing presence of Jesus.

∞ links

Read about verses 16:9–20 on pages 70–71.

C *The Church of the Resurrection, said to be on the site of Jesus' tomb*

Discussion activity 👥

In pairs or small groups, discuss the debate about the ending of Mark's Gospel at 16:8. Do you think it is an appropriate ending to the gospel? If so, explain why. If not, what do you think of the suggestions that have been made as to why it might have ended at this point?

Study tip

A question testing knowledge of Mark 16:1–8 is a frequent one in exam. If asked to give an account of this incident, make sure that you do not include material from other gospels.

Summary

You should now know and understand Mark's account of the empty tomb and the debate relating to the ending of his gospel at verse 16:8.

3.11 Jesus' Resurrection (2)

■ The Resurrection appearances (Mark 16:9–20)

For most Christians, the Resurrection of Jesus is the keystone of their faith, confirming their beliefs about Jesus and giving them hope of eternal life. Very early on, some Christians seem to have felt that because the account of Jesus' life in Mark's Gospel led up to his Resurrection, the gospel ought to end with an account of Jesus' Resurrection appearances. The written style of these verses differs from the rest of the gospel and it appears that they were added later. Although the author's identity is not known, it is likely that the verses were written in the early 2nd century CE, as they were known to Christians writing in the middle of that century.

Appearance to Mary Magdalene

> **Beliefs and teachings**
>
> When Jesus rose early on the first day of the week, he appeared first to Mary Magdalene, out of whom he had driven seven demons. She went and told those who had been with him and who were mourning and weeping. When they heard that Jesus was alive and that she had seen him, they did not believe it.
>
> *Mark 16:9–11*

Mark's Gospel gives us little information about Mary Magdalene – see the Links opposite for information on the references to her. Yet Mary is the only one of the women mentioned whose name remains exactly the same in all the references. This suggests that she had a firm place in the early Christian tradition. Again, it is significant that Jesus' first appearance was to a woman, in view of their status in 1st-century Israel. The disciples' lack of faith is emphasised.

Appearance to two disciples

Again, there is the theme of disbelief. Although these verses were not written by Mark, they fit in with the theme of discipleship, which is a key theme in the gospel. Several times Jesus' disciples lacked understanding or faith during Jesus' ministry.

The commission

> **Beliefs and teachings**
>
> Later Jesus appeared to the Eleven as they were eating; he rebuked them for their lack of faith and their stubborn refusal to believe those who had seen him after he had risen. He said to them, 'Go into all the world and preach the good news to all creation. Whoever believes and is baptised will be saved, but whoever does not believe will be condemned. And these signs will accompany those who believe: In my name they will drive out demons; they will speak in new tongues; they will pick up snakes with their hands; and when they drink deadly poison, it will not hurt them at all; they will place their hands on sick people, and they will get well.'
>
> *Mark 16:14–18*

Objectives

Study the Resurrection appearances recorded in Mark 16:9–20.

A *St Mary Magdalene Church in Jerusalem, one of many dedicated to Mary Magdalene*

⚭ links

Read what information Mark does give about Mary Magdalene in Mark 15:40–41, 47 and 16:1–8.

> **Beliefs and teachings**
>
> Afterwards Jesus appeared in a different form to two of them while they were walking in the country. These returned and reported it to the rest; but they did not believe them either.
>
> *Mark 16:12–13*

⚭ links

To read about the significance for Mark's readers of the theme of the disciples' failure, see pages 18–19.

After telling the Eleven off for their lack of faith, Jesus gave them the authority to preach the good news throughout the world, known as the **commission**. These verses also refer to other practices found in early Christian communities. The disciples had already carried out exorcism (driving out demons) and healing when Jesus had sent them out on a mission. There are many New Testament references to speaking in tongues. Some Christians went into a trance-like state and made unintelligible sounds. This 'speech' was thought to be inspired by the Holy Spirit. When shipwrecked on Malta, Paul picked up a snake and was unharmed. The ability to drink deadly poison without harm is not mentioned in the New Testament but was claimed in other early Christian writings. Some of these things are still practised, mainly by Pentecostal Christians.

Key terms

Commission: the occasion, after the Resurrection, when the risen Jesus told the Eleven to preach the good news to the whole world.

⚭ links

For healings by Peter, Acts 3:1–8; for speaking in tongues, Acts 2:1–4; for Paul in Malta, Acts 28:1–6; for the commission, pages 124–125.

Case study

Pentecostal churches

Christians who belong to Pentecostal churches put great emphasis on the work of the Holy Spirit. They take literally the words of Mark 16:17–18 and during their services they practise speaking in tongues. A few churches in the US practise snake handling, even though some of the worshippers have died of snake bites. They also have prayer cloths. Healers pray over them before passing them on to sick people, who put them against the part of the body that is suffering.

Activity

1   a   Read the information about Pentecostal churches in the case study above.

   b   How do the practices described link up with Jesus' commission?

B   *Although illegal, some churches in the US still practise snake handling during worship*

The Ascension

Beliefs and teachings

After the Lord Jesus had spoken to them, he was taken up into heaven and he sat at the right hand of God. Then the disciples went out and preached everywhere, and the Lord worked with them and confirmed his word by the signs that accompanied it.

Mark 16:19–20

The Ascension, when Jesus returned to God in heaven, marked the end of Jesus' physical presence on earth. For early Christian communities, it was the final proof that Jesus was, indeed, the Son of God. While Jesus was no longer physically with the disciples, Mark explained that he continued to work with them. He became a *spiritual* presence in their lives. For believers, the Ascension showed that Jesus was king.

C   *Church of the Ascension, Moscow: many churches are dedicated to the Ascension*

Summary

By now you should know the stories of the Resurrection appearances recorded in Mark's Gospel.

Study tip

These verses are a summary of a number of Resurrection appearances and it is important that you know about and understand the different events described in them.

What does the Resurrection mean for Christians?

Right from the start of the Church, the death and resurrection of Jesus were key elements in Christian preaching. The most important day in the Christian year is Easter Sunday, the day when Christians remember the Resurrection. Because Jesus was raised to life on a Sunday, Christians made Sunday their holy day. The Resurrection means a number of things for Christians, explored below.

A living Christ Christians worship a living Christ, not a crucified martyr. The Resurrection brought Jesus back to life, and the Ascension created a living **spiritual** presence in the lives of Christians.

Teaching that can be trusted On many occasions Jesus referred to his future suffering, death and resurrection. Christians believe that all his teaching can be trusted, as these predictions came true.

A sign of God's power Christians believe that God did the apparently impossible in raising Jesus to life, an indication of God's power. Nothing is too great for God to achieve, and this is comforting and encouraging for Christians in difficulty.

Death is not the end Christians see Jesus' death and resurrection as opening the possibility of eternal life with God, to be enjoyed in its fullness after death. Death is not something to be feared, but simply the gateway to a new and richer form of life. This is a comfort to Christians facing death or grieving for the death of loved ones. They believe that the separation is not final, and that those who have died are with God.

A sign of victory over all evil Through the Resurrection, Christians believe that life has triumphed over death, good over evil, hope over despair. Whatever sufferings they undergo in life, they can be sure that in the end nothing can separate them from God's love.

The resurrection life can be lived in the present Baptism is a symbol of rebirth, and many Christians practise this, believing that at their baptism they receive gifts that enable them to live in a new relationship with God. They can begin to experience the resurrection life that will be fully theirs after death. This has an impact on their lifestyle. In some churches on Easter Sunday, a New Testament passage is read – given in the Beliefs and teachings box on the right – that makes it clear what this means.

Objectives

Explore the significance of the Resurrection for Christians.

Consider arguments for and against its historical truth.

A *Christians believe death is not the end*

Research activity

The Scillitan martyrs

1 In July 180 CE a number of North African Christians were martyred. Search the internet for the official Roman transcript of their trial and a Christian comment at the end. How did belief in the Resurrection influence these men and women at their trial?

Beliefs and teachings

Since, then, you have been raised with Christ, set your hearts on things above ... Therefore, as God's chosen people ... clothe yourselves with compassion, kindness, humility, gentleness and patience ... Forgive as the Lord forgave you. And over all these virtues put on love ...

Colossians 3:1, 12–14

■ Symbols of the Resurrection

■ Did the Resurrection really happen?

Read the arguments for and against the Resurrection being a historical reality in the table below.

B   *A symbol of the Resurrection – what is the significance of such symbols to Christians?*

Yes	No
Mark was inspired by God, so it must be true.	Mark was a human capable of making mistakes, as were his sources.
God's power overrides the laws of nature.	Rising from the dead is impossible; it contradicts the laws of nature.
If the story was untrue, its author would not have included the unlikely detail that women were witnesses.	It may be that its author had a purpose that cannot now be known.
The women noted where Jesus' body was buried.	Maybe the women went to the wrong tomb.
The story of the empty tomb is very restrained; a made-up story would have been much more dramatic.	Perhaps the story of the empty tomb was a kind of parable, making the point that Jesus would never be forgotten.
The centurion would not have made a mistake; Jesus was dead. Jesus could not have moved after his physical ordeal.	Perhaps Jesus was not dead but unconscious. The appearances could have been of a revived rather than a resurrected Jesus.
It is unlikely that his body was moved: the disciples were too afraid, and the Jews and Romans had no reason to move it. If they had, they would have used his body to discredit stories of the Resurrection.	His body might have been moved by his disciples, who wished to honour it. Or the Jews or Romans might have wanted to prevent his memory being honoured, so took the body away.
The disciples' lack of faith and their need of forgiveness is emphasised throughout Mark 16. The disciples, lacking faith, would not have made the Resurrection story up.	The Resurrection appearances might have been a form of wishful thinking to make up for their lack of faith.
The disciples changed from being afraid into courageous preachers of the gospel. Something special must have happened.	The Resurrection appearances might have been hallucinations, one reported 'sighting' sparking off another.
Most of the Eleven died as martyrs – they would not have given their lives for what they knew was a lie.	Perhaps the Eleven became so involved in the lie that they started to believe it or did not know how to get out of it without losing face.

Summary

By now you should understand the significance for Christians of belief in the Resurrection, and be able to evaluate some of the arguments for and against its historical truth.

3

Jesus' suffering, death and Resurrection – summary

For the examination, you should now be able to:

✔ describe the following events
  – the entry into Jerusalem (Mark 11:1–11)
  – the anointing at Bethany (Mark 14:1–11)
  – the Last Supper (Mark 14:12–25)
  – Jesus in Gethsemane (Mark 14:32–52)
  – the trials before the Sanhedrin (Jewish Council) and Pilate (Mark 14:53–65; 15:1–20)

✔ understand the significance of these events for Jesus, his disciples and for Christians

✔ give an account of the crucifixion and burial (Mark 15:21–47), and understand the meaning for Christians of Jesus' death

✔ describe Mark's account of the empty tomb (Mark 16:1–8) and Resurrection appearances (Mark 16:9–20), and the meaning for Christians of the Resurrection

✔ understand the debate about the ending of Mark's Gospel at 16:8 and the historical value of the Resurrection stories.

Sample answer

1   Write an answer to the following exam question:

'Pilate was mainly to blame for Jesus' death.' Do you agree? Give reasons for your answer, showing that you have thought about more than one point of view.   (6 marks)

2   a   Read the sample answer below:

> The account of Jesus' trial shows that Pilate thought Jesus was innocent, yet he did not set him free. Instead he tried to pass the responsibility onto the crowd by giving them the choice. This was a cowardly thing to do. He knew people hated Jesus and he wanted to remain popular. If he had freed Jesus, there would probably have been trouble, and Pilate's job might have been threatened. He certainly didn't want that. So he put his own interests first. He had the power to enforce justice and should have done so. If there had been trouble, he had soldiers at hand to deal with it. Pilate certainly should take most of the blame. He was the one who sentenced Jesus to death, and who ordered the flogging and the crucifixion.

   b   With a partner, discuss the sample answer. It contains a serious weakness. What is it?

   c   What mark would you give this answer out of 6? Look at the mark scheme in the Introduction on page 7 (AO2). What are the reasons for the mark you have given?

Practice questions

A *At Holy Communion, Christians remember Jesus' words and actions at the Last Supper*

1 At the Last Supper, what did Jesus say and do in connection with:
   (a) the bread   *(3 marks)*
   (b) the wine?   *(3 marks)*

2 What did Jesus say during the Last Supper about the person who would betray him?   *(2 marks)*

3 Give an account of Jesus' arrest.   *(6 marks)*

4 'Jesus was at his weakest in Gethsemane.' Do you agree? Give reasons for your answer, showing that you have thought about more than one point of view.   *(6 marks)*

> **Study tip** Remember, for an evaluation question carrying 6 marks, when asked if you agree with a statement, you must give reasons for your opinion. You will not gain any marks just for saying that you agree or disagree with something.

> **Study tip** When you give your opinion in a 6-mark evaluation question, you must say why others might not agree. A one-sided answer can only achieve 4 marks. An answer with no religious comment will achieve no more than 3 marks.

4.1 Jesus the teacher and miracle worker

Introduction

For Mark, Jesus' teaching and miracle working could not be separated. In his accounts of many of the miracles, Mark refers to Jesus' role and authority as a teacher. Likewise, Mark used Jesus' miracles to shed light on his teachings and people's responses, such as in the link between Jesus' healing of a blind man and the teaching at Caesarea Philippi. The Person of Jesus is revealed in his roles as teacher and miracle worker.

Jesus the teacher

Mark states on many occasions that Jesus was teaching. People often called him a rabbi, meaning teacher. There were many rabbis in Israel. Some, like Jesus, travelled around the towns and villages, delivering their teaching. Once, those listening to Jesus were stunned by the difference between his teaching and that of the rabbis they usually heard. The rabbis usually based their teaching on that of the great rabbis, and said nothing new. Jesus had received no rabbinic training, but he taught with the kind of authority that only the most notable rabbis had. Mark clearly saw this authority as given by God.

Like the rabbis of his day, Jesus used parables to make his points. Parables were illustrations from, or stories about, everyday life that contained a deeper meaning. His audience would have found them interesting, memorable and challenging, for the points he made in them were not always obvious.

Objectives

Explore Mark's portrayal of Jesus as teacher and miracle worker.

Consider these roles as pointers to the Person of Jesus.

links

Remind yourself of the link between the healing of the blind man and Jesus' teaching at Caesarea Philippi on page 44.

links

Read more about the parables of Jesus on pages 126–127.

Activity

1. Create a table entitled 'Jesus as teacher' with three columns.

   Head the first column 'Bible reference', and then enter the following set text references from Mark's Gospel, allowing a row for each: 4:35–38; 5:35; 9:2–5; 10:17, 20; 12:13–14, 28–32; 14:12–14, 43–45.

   Head the second column 'Person(s) speaking', and then enter the identity of the person(s) who referred to Jesus as teacher or rabbi in each of the Bible references.

   Head the third column 'Context', and enter the context in which the words were spoken. You might find that the headings to these Bible passages help you with this.

   For instance, in 4:35–38, the disciples were those who used the word 'teacher' and the context is that this happened in the story of Jesus calming the storm.

Extension activity

Mark 1:21–28 is not a set text, but reading it will add to your understanding of Jesus' authority as a teacher.

A *An icon portraying Jesus the teacher*

■ Jesus the miracle worker

In the 1st century, there were many who travelled throughout the Mediterranean world including Israel, claiming to perform miracles. According to Mark, Jesus was able to perform different kinds of miracles: healings, exorcisms (driving out demons) and nature miracles.

Healings

Mark describes Jesus curing people of their disabilities or healing their diseases. Once, what started out as the healing of a sick child ended up with her raised from the dead. These stories often portray Jesus as showing compassion as well as power. Usually Mark ended his accounts of Jesus' healings with a reference to the amazement of those who were there. These witnesses usually commented on Jesus' authority and power.

Exorcisms

In the ancient world, mental illness and some physical conditions were thought to be due to demons entering people's bodies and taking control of both their personalities and their physical behaviour. According to Mark's Gospel, Jesus' ability to perform exorcisms was not disputed, but opinions differed as to where his power came from. Ordinary people saw it as a sign of Jesus' authority from God. Those who were possessed by demons often declared Jesus to be a supernatural being, and Jesus silenced them. This was part of the Messianic Secret. However, the scribes sent from Jerusalem to investigate Jesus decided that he was in league with Satan.

Nature miracles

According to Mark, on a number of occasions, Jesus defied the laws of nature. He saved his disciples by calming a storm on the Sea of Galilee; he came to his disciples on the same lake by walking across its waters; and he fed a huge crowd with a tiny amount of food. Such miracles were intended as pointers to Jesus' God-given power. As in the healings, those present usually commented on his power and their amazement at what they had witnessed.

B   *This stained glass window depicts Jesus healing a sick man*

∞ links

Read more about the Messianic Secret on pages 84–85.

∞ links

Read more about Jesus' miracles on pages 24–25, 78–79 and 96–97.

Activity

2   Answer the following questions from memory, then use these pages to check your answers.

   a   Name three types of miracle that Jesus performed, according to Mark's Gospel.

   b   What do the healing miracles show about Jesus?

   c   How did opinions differ over the exorcisms performed by Jesus?

   d   What are nature miracles?

   e   Name two nature miracles recorded in Mark's Gospel.

Study tip

When reading Mark's accounts of Jesus' miracles, look behind the stories to what they teach about the Person of Jesus, as you might be required to do this in the exam.

Summary

You should now know that Mark's Gospel presents Jesus as both a teacher and miracle worker. You should have some understanding of how these roles pointed to his authority and power.

The feeding of the five thousand (1)

■ The feeding of the five thousand (Mark 6:30–44)

The apostles gathered around Jesus and reported to him all they had done and taught. Then, because so many people were coming and going that they did not even have a chance to eat, he said to them, 'Come with me by yourselves to a quiet place and get some rest.'

So they went away by themselves in a boat to a solitary place. But many who saw them leaving recognized them and ran on foot from all the towns and got there ahead of them. When Jesus landed and saw a large crowd, he had compassion on them, because they were like sheep without a shepherd. So he began teaching them many things.

By this time it was late in the day, so his disciples came to him. 'This is a remote place,' they said, 'and it's already very late. Send the people away so that they can go to the surrounding countryside and villages and buy themselves something to eat.'

But he answered, 'You give them something to eat.'

They said to him, 'That would take almost a year's wages! Are we to go and spend that much on bread and give it to them to eat?'

'How many loaves do you have?' he asked. 'Go and see.'

When they found out, they said, 'Five – and two fish.'

Then Jesus directed them to have all the people sit down in groups on the green grass. So they sat down in groups of hundreds and fifties. Taking the five loaves and the two fish and looking up to heaven, he gave thanks and broke the loaves. Then he gave them to his disciples to set before the people. He also divided the two fish among them all. They all ate and were satisfied, and the disciples picked up twelve basketfuls of broken pieces of bread and fish. The number of the men who had eaten was five thousand.

Mark 6:30–44

Objectives

Study the story of the feeding of the five thousand and understand the symbolism behind its details.

Explore Jesus' roles as teacher, miracle worker and Messiah.

A *Mark thought of Jesus as being like a shepherd guiding his flock*

This story, which brings together Jesus' roles as teacher and miracle worker, is told more often in the New Testament than any other miracle story. Mark records two versions of it, as well as teaching relating to it. For Mark and the early Christian community, this miracle had great significance.

As with many stories recorded by Mark, there is a wealth of Old Testament reference. Without understanding this, the miracle's deeper significance cannot fully be understood. Modern writers have often been concerned with what actually happened, and their suggestions will be considered. But what is really important for many Christians is not what happened but what the story **means**.

Moses said to the Lord, 'May the Lord ... appoint a man over this community ... one who will lead them out and bring them in, so that the Lord's people will not be like sheep without a shepherd.'

Numbers 27:15–17

Discussion activity

Read through Mark 6:30–34 and this page again. In pairs, discuss the ways in which Mark portrays different aspects of Jesus' character and Christian beliefs about his true identity.

Jesus the teacher

Jesus had sent out the Twelve on a preaching and healing mission. They had now returned and Jesus took them away from the crowds to relax. They sailed across the Sea of Galilee, hoping for peace and quiet, but people who saw them leave guessed where they were making for. When Jesus arrived, he was met again by a large crowd. Recognising that they were desperate for spiritual guidance, Jesus reacted with compassion, not irritation, and taught them for many hours. Mark referred to them as sheep without a shepherd. Several Old Testament passages used the metaphor of shepherd for the future Messiah. So Mark was pointing beyond Jesus' role as teacher to his identity as Messiah.

Jesus the miracle worker

Jesus' disciples eventually told him to send off the crowd to buy food. When Jesus told the disciples to give the people food, they were understandably stunned to be asked to feed such a large crowd. Told to see how much food they had, they returned with five round loaves and two salted fish. Some scholars see these numbers as standing for the five books of the Jewish Law and the two stone tablets on which the Ten Commandments were said to have been written.

The people were told to sit in groups of hundreds or fifties. (The reference to the green grass suggests it was springtime.) It is unlikely that the disciples could have organised so many people in this way, so the reference may instead reflect how some remembered what happened. In Old Testament times, hundreds and fifties were army units. Perhaps some felt they were like an army, ready to march behind Jesus.

As was the custom at a meal, Jesus took the bread, gave thanks to God and broke the bread, before giving it to the disciples to be shared out. The words used here are very close to those used at the Last Supper. Mark might well have intended to make a link with that event and the Eucharist (Holy Communion).

All those who ate were full, and despite the size of the crowd there were leftovers to fill twelve baskets. The number twelve was symbolic of the twelve tribes that formed Israel, God's chosen people. Mark was perhaps referring to Jesus the teacher as well as the miracle worker, stating that what he gave was more than enough for those who followed him and became part of the new Israel. For Mark these two roles of teacher and miracle worker were part of Jesus' overall role as Messiah.

∞ links

Read about the mission of the Twelve on pages 120–121.

B   *A mosaic in the church at Tabgha on the shores of Lake Galilee, traditionally the place where this miracle occurred*

∞ links

Read more about the significance of this miracle, pages 80–81; the title Messiah, pages 82–85; and the Last Supper, pages 54–55.

Activity

Read through Mark 6:35–44 and these pages again. Then from memory describe what happened. You need not include any of the explanation given of the details. Check what you have written with the text, and make any amendments to improve your account.

Summary

You should now know in detail the story of the feeding of the five thousand, and understand the symbolism contained in it and how Mark uses it to portray the Person of Jesus.

Study tip

Look behind the details of this story to see how Mark portrays Jesus.

■ Different views

Some Christians believe that if Jesus was, indeed, the Son of God, then nothing was impossible for him. They also believe that since Mark's Gospel was divinely inspired, it always tells the historical truth and this miracle, therefore, occurred exactly as Mark recorded it. Others think that a miracle did happen, but that the number of those fed has been exaggerated. It has also been suggested that because of their strict food laws, most people in the crowd would have taken food with them. When they saw that Jesus and his disciples were prepared to share what they had, these people were shamed into doing the same.

Many Christians, however, believe that something out of the ordinary did happen but that it is not possible to know exactly what because of the influence of Old Testament stories on the way the story was relayed. They, therefore, look for a **symbolic** meaning in the story. Some of the key symbolic features of the story are explored below.

Manna in the wilderness

According to the Old Testament, after escaping from Egypt, Moses and the Israelites wandered for many years through the wilderness, a harsh and infertile land. Often they were hungry, but God always provided. Every morning the Israelites found a white sugary substance on the ground. They asked, 'What is it?', to which Moses replied, 'It is the bread the Lord has given you to eat.' Their question gave this substance its name: manna (which in Hebrew means 'What is it?'). Each day there was enough, and it became a symbol for Jews of God's generosity. Many looked for the coming of a Messiah who, like Moses, would again feed people with manna. Manna was also a symbol of the Torah. So symbolically, at the feeding of this great crowd, Jesus the Messiah provided the crowd with manna in his roles as both teacher and miracle worker. He gave them the physical and spiritual 'food' they needed to survive, and the teachings continue to provide this for Christians today.

Objectives

Explore different views about what happened at the feeding of the five thousand.

Consider what Christians learn from this miracle about the Person of Jesus, and its continuing importance for Christians today.

Beliefs and teachings

That evening quail came and covered the camp, and in the morning there was a layer of dew around the camp. When the dew was gone, thin flakes like frost on the ground appeared on the desert floor. When the Israelites saw it, they said to each other, 'What is it?' For they did not know what it was.

Moses said to them, 'It is the bread the LORD has given you to eat. This is what the LORD has commanded: "Each one is to gather as much as he needs. Take an omer for each person you have in your tent."'

Exodus 16:13–16

A   *The Israelites spent 40 years in the wilderness*

The Messianic banquet

Linked to the story of manna is the image of the Messianic banquet. This is a symbol of the joy that Jews would experience when the Messiah came, initiating the Kingdom of God. This miracle shows Jesus the Messiah offering his people a banquet, both physically and spiritually.

The Eucharist

The words used to describe Jesus' actions with the loaves are similar to those spoken at the Last Supper. Mark might have seen this incident as pointing forward to the Eucharist (Holy Communion). Some Christians think that Jesus himself had in mind the sacred meal that he would one day institute, and that what each person received here was a tiny fragment of food.

Christians today believe that when they receive Holy Communion, they are spiritually fed and filled with the living presence of Jesus, so that they are strengthened to serve God in the world.

◯◯ links

Read Jesus' words about the bread at the Last Supper in Mark 14:22, or pages 54–55.

◼ The Person of Jesus

The feeding of the five thousand portrays Jesus as teacher and miracle worker, but for many Christians it is more significant than that. They, like Mark, see the miracle as pointing to Jesus as the long-expected Messiah. They believe it shows him fulfilling his people's needs, feeding them spiritually with his teaching. They also think it presents him as the powerful Son of God, who is able to suspend the laws of nature.

Activity

Write an explanation of the symbolism behind the story of the feeding of the five thousand. Use Mark 6:30–44, along with pages 78–81 of this book to help you. Write an additional paragraph on what the story teaches about the Person of Jesus.

Discussion activity 👥

1 a   In pairs, consider the various explanations for this story given above. Discuss the different suggestions as to what might have happened and the view that the strong Old Testament influence on Mark's account makes it impossible to know what occurred.

   b   Which of these views, if any, make the most sense to you, and why?

   c   Do you think it matters to Christians if the story actually happened?

Study tip

Think carefully about what can be learned from this story about the Person of Jesus, and why the story is important to Christians today.

Summary

You should now understand what Christians learn about the Person of Jesus in the story of the feeding of the five thousand, and its importance for Christians today.

B *Jesus broke the bread when he fed the crowd and at the Last Supper*

4.4 Titles for Jesus: Christ/Messiah (1)

Introduction

The early Christians tried to show their beliefs about Jesus by giving him titles. There are many titles for Jesus in Mark's Gospel. Three of these are set for study: Christ/Messiah, Son of Man and Son of God. See the Links opposite for details of where to find information on each of them.

Christ/Messiah: the Jewish background

An anointed one

Christ is not Jesus' surname but the Greek translation of the Hebrew term **Messiah.** (Most early Christians read the Old Testament in Greek and did not understand Hebrew.) Messiah means 'anointed one'. In the Old Testament this title was used especially of kings. Anointing (pouring oil on someone's head) was a sign that God had chosen them. It set them apart from ordinary people, and they were meant to make sure that people lived as God wanted, and to pray to God on their behalf.

A king descended from King David

Discussion activity

Discuss in pairs or small groups the characteristics that you would expect a king to possess, such as authority, wealth or power. Of the list you create, which do you think are the most important and why?

Although he had faults, King David ruled well, but most of the kings who followed him did not. They were often greedy and unjust. So the prophets (men believed to be chosen by God to declare his will) began to look forward to a time in the future when this would change. They thought God would send a king who would bring justice and peace – see the Beliefs and teachings box. They referred to him as 'the anointed one', and because David was such a good king, they thought he would be descended from him. Because of this, the Messiah was sometimes given another title: Son of David.

> **Beliefs and teachings**
>
> For to us a child is born,
> to us a son is given,
> and the government will be on his shoulders.
> And he will be called
> Wonderful Counsellor, Mighty God,
> Everlasting Father, Prince of Peace.
>
> *Isaiah 9:6*

Objectives

Explore Old Testament and 1st-century Jewish ideas about the nature and role of the Messiah.

⊙⊙ links

For more on Christ/Messiah, read pages 84–85; for Son of Man, pages 86–89; for Son of God, 90–91.

> **Key terms**
>
> **Christ:** the leader promised by God to the Jews. The word literally means 'Anointed One' in Greek; the Hebrew equivalent is Messiah. Christians believe Jesus to be the Christ.
>
> **Messiah:** the person whom God will send to save humanity, believed by Christians to be Jesus (the Anointed One). Hebrew form of the word 'Christ'.

A *At Christmas, many choirs sing 'Messiah' by Handel*

B *David captured Jerusalem to make it Israel's capital city*

C *David was Israel's greatest king and some of the Old Testament psalms are attributed to him*

A supernatural figure

Eventually the monarchy came to an end, so beliefs about the Messiah changed. Many Jews began to think instead of a supernatural figure sent by God. A new age would begin, and everyone would accept God's authority.

A warrior

Many 1st-century Jews hoped for a leader who would set the Jews free from the Romans and establish Israel as an independent nation once more. The Zealots, in particular, looked for a warrior Messiah. Throughout Jesus' life there were men who claimed to be the Messiah; they led Zealot uprisings that were put down by the Romans.

Activity

1   Read through these pages again, then answer the questions below. When you have finished, check that your answers are correct.

   a   Why were kings anointed?

   b   Why did the prophets begin to look to the future rather than to the current king for the fulfilment of their hopes about a Messiah?

   c   Why did most Jews believe that the Messiah would be a descendant of King David?

   d   What characteristics did the prophets expect the Messiah to possess?

   e   Why did many Jews of Jesus' day hope for a warrior Messiah?

∞ links

For more about anointing see pages 50–51; for the Zealots, see pages 32–33.

Summary

You should now understand some different Old Testament and 1st-century Jewish ideas about the role of the Messiah, to help you to understand Jesus' attitude to it as a title for him and its relevance for Christians.

Study tip

It is important that you know the background to the role and nature of the Messiah. This will help you to understand Jesus' attitude to it as a title and to assess its relevance to modern Christianity.

Introduction

⚭links

See pages 82–83 for the Jewish background to the titles 'Christ' and 'Messiah' before working through these pages.

Having explored the background to the titles 'Christ' and 'Messiah', these pages will examine Jesus' own attitude to these titles, and what they mean to Christians today.

The Messianic Secret

Jesus only once used the title Messiah of himself in private conversation with his disciples. The overall impression of Mark's Gospel is that for most of his ministry Jesus seems to have discouraged its use. He did not want people referring to him as Messiah when they were discussing him with one another. When he performed miracles, he often told people not to tell others about them. This is because many Jews expected the Messiah to be able to perform miracles as proof of who he was and Jesus did not heal people to prove his identity. The Messianic Secret is an important theme that runs right through Mark's Gospel, as the following examples show.

Caesarea Philippi

⚭links

Read this set text in Mark 8:27–33 or on page 42 before working through the rest of this section.

When Jesus asked the disciples who people thought he was, they made several suggestions, such as Elijah. When asked who **they** thought he was, however, Peter declared, 'You are the Messiah'. Jesus immediately gave his disciples strict instructions to keep this a secret. Several reasons have been suggested for why he did this. Many Jews thought the Messiah would be a king with great wealth and power, demanding obedience and service. Jesus' ministry shows that this was not his aim. He wanted people to come to their own conclusions about him. In the tense situation of that time, those who were oppressed wanted a political saviour, someone to set them free from Roman rule. That was not Jesus' aim, either. Moreover, the Romans knew that peace in Israel was very fragile. Pilate and his officials were constantly watching for unrest. The Sanhedrin, anxious to please the Romans, would probably have warned Pilate of any potential troublemaker and he would have been arrested and his ministry would have come to an end at a very early stage. Jesus wanted time to teach both the crowds and his disciples before this happened.

Objectives

Study the use of the title Christ/Messiah in Mark's Gospel and to explore Jesus' attitude to Messiah as a title for him.

Explore modern Christian views on the importance of the title 'Messiah'.

A *Jesus did not see himself as an earthly powerful king*

Activities

1. Read the following Bible texts: Mark 1:40–45; 5:35–43; 8:27–33; 9:2–9. All apart from 9:9 are set texts.

2. Write a paragraph giving possible reasons why Jesus did not want his identity as Messiah to be widely known. You should support what you write by referring to at least three of the texts you have studied.

The final stages of Jesus' ministry

Towards the end of his ministry, Jesus seems to have been less concerned about the use of the title, perhaps because he knew that his ministry was drawing to a close. When Bartimaeus (a blind man) repeatedly called him 'Son of David', Jesus did not silence him. His decision to ride into Jerusalem on a colt was a way of showing the kind of Messiah he was. Above all, at the trial before the Sanhedrin, when the high priest asked, 'Are you the Messiah?', Jesus replied, 'I am', though he went on to refer to himself as 'Son of Man'.

∞ links

Read about Bartimaeus on pages 114–115; and Jesus' entry into Jerusalem and trial on pages 50–51 and 58–59 to help you with this section.

■ The title 'Messiah' and modern Christianity

Today, people often refer to Jesus as Christ without thinking of its meaning. Strictly speaking, they should say 'Jesus the Christ'. Many Christians like the title Messiah for Jesus. It reminds them that Jesus was a historical figure, a descendant of David. It also reminds them that he fulfilled Old Testament predictions of a leader who would think about others, promoting justice and peace. For Christians, Jesus is their king.

Other Christians, however, prefer different titles for Jesus. For them, Messiah is a Jewish title, and few Christians have a Jewish background to help them to fully appreciate it. They also feel that to call Jesus Messiah might encourage misunderstanding. Status and power are important to people nowadays, and this title might encourage them to think of Jesus as a worldly king.

B *Statue in Lisbon of Christ as king*

Summary

You should now understand Jesus' views on the title Christ, or Messiah. You should also understand differing Christian views on its significance as a title for Jesus.

Titles for Jesus: Son of Man (1)

Introduction

Like 'Messiah', **'Son of Man'** is a Jewish title with its background in the Old Testament. Its various meanings are explored below.

Son of Man: the Old Testament background

A man

In the psalms, 'son of man' is simply another way of saying 'a man' or 'humanity'. For example, Psalm 8 is a hymn celebrating the wonders of the universe and praising God as the Creator. In this psalm, the author described humanity as insignificant when compared with the vastness of the heavens, yet having a special place in the universe. In this psalm, 'son of man' is a synonym for 'man', i.e. human being.

Beliefs and teachings

When I consider your heavens,
the work of your fingers …
what is man that you are mindful of him,
the son of man that you care for him?

Psalms 8:3–4

A *In the vastness of the universe, what is the role of human beings?*

A vulnerable human being

The book of Ezekiel contains the writings of a prophet in the 6th century BCE. Ezekiel had many visions in which God gave him teachings and messages for the Jews among whom he lived. In these visions, God always referred to Ezekiel as 'son of man'. It was a way of making a contrast between the power and majesty of God and the human weakness of Ezekiel. Compared with God, humans were weak, vulnerable creatures.

Objectives

Explore the ways in which the title 'Son of Man' was used in both the Old Testament and in Mark's Gospel.

Consider possible reasons why Jesus preferred it to the title Messiah.

Key terms

Son of Man: a title used by Jesus of himself. In the Old Testament, the title was used of a heavenly being from God. Jesus used the title to stress that he was more than simply a human being and that he came with authority from God. Jesus also linked the title with suffering and service.

Beliefs and teachings

This was the appearance of the likeness of the glory of the Lord. When I saw it, I fell face down, and I heard the voice of one speaking. He said to me, 'Son of man, stand up on your feet and I will speak to you.' As he spoke, the Spirit came into me and raised me to my feet …

Ezekiel 1:28–2:2

A glorious being

Much of the Old Testament book of Daniel consists of a series of visions, full of symbolic language. It was written at a time of great crisis, when there was an attempt to destroy the Jewish religion. Daniel's visions stated that God would step in, the present age would come to an end and a new age would begin. In one of his visions, the author referred to a son of man being given authority by God over all the nations of the world. The important points to note here are that the term Son of Man is associated with glory, power and authority and the message that God would save those who suffered.

■ Son of Man in Mark's Gospel

The title 'Son of Man' occurs on 14 occasions in Mark's Gospel. According to Mark, it was the title Jesus used of himself. It was used by no one else. It is, therefore, very important, and shows how Jesus wanted to be understood. Some scholars claim that in the 1st century, in the time of Jesus, Son of Man simply meant 'I'. Jesus used the title to refer to his ministry, his suffering and his future glory. Perhaps he liked this title because it was vague or because, if challenged, he could have argued that it simply meant a man. It could mean many things and, unlike Messiah, had no links to political kingship. He could, therefore, use it without risk of misunderstanding and arrest while still linking himself to the Old Testament references.

Beliefs and teachings

'In my vision at night I looked, and there before me was one like a son of man, coming with the clouds of heaven. He approached the Ancient of Days and was led into his presence. He was given authority, glory and sovereign power; all peoples … worshipped him.'

Daniel 7:13–14

Beliefs and teachings

'…the Son of Man has authority on earth to forgive sins.'

Mark 2:10

He then began to teach them that the Son of Man must suffer many things and be rejected by the elders, the chief priests and the teachers of the law, and that he must be killed and after three days rise again.

Mark 8:31

'For even the Son of Man did not come to be served, but to serve, and to give his life as a ransom for many.'

Mark 10:45

Activities

1 Read through these pages on the Jewish background to the title Son of Man. Then, from memory, write two or three sentences on each of the three ways in which this title was used. When you have done this, check that what you have written is correct.

2 This task is intended to help you with three things:
   ■ to introduce you to all the set texts where the title is used;
   ■ to help you see the three ways in which Jesus used the title;
   ■ to help when you come to revise for tests or for the exam by ensuring you have all the Son of Man references in one place.

   a Copy out each of the following set texts: Mark 2:10; 8:31; 10:45; 14:21, 62.

   b Decide which of the following headings is most appropriate to each use of the title 'Son of Man': 'Teaching and healing', 'Suffering', or 'Future glory'.

Study tip

Make sure that you know the three different ways in which Jesus used the title Son of Man. In an exam you might be asked to explain why this title was important for Jesus.

Extension activity

Add the following texts to the list you have created: Mark 2:28; 8:38; 9:9, 12, 31; 10:33; 13:26.

These are not set texts, but they will give you a broader picture of Mark's use of the title. You could use this additional information in an exam.

Summary

You should now know different ways in which 'Son of Man' was used in the Old Testament and in Mark's Gospel. You should also understand why Jesus preferred it as a title.

Titles for Jesus: Son of Man (2)

■ Introduction

⊚links

Read pages 86–87 for the background on Jesus' use of the term Son of Man.

You have learned that Jesus used the title Son of Man in three ways: to refer to his ministry, his suffering and his future glory. These pages explain those three uses in more detail.

■ 'Son of Man' in Jesus' ministry (Mark 2:1–12)

On two occasions, Jesus used the title 'Son of Man' in relation to his ministry, linking it with ideas of God-given authority in response to criticism by religious leaders. The first occasion, the healing of a paralysed man, is a set text and is examined in detail below. You can study the second occasion and extend your knowledge and understanding by completing the Extension activity.

The paralysed man

Beliefs and teachings

A few days later, when Jesus again entered Capernaum, the people heard that he had come home. They gathered in such large numbers that there was no room left, not even outside the door, and he preached the word to them. Some men came, bringing to him a paralysed man, carried by four of them. Since they could not get him to Jesus because of the crowd, they made an opening in the roof above Jesus by digging through it and then lowered the mat the man was lying on. When Jesus saw their faith, he said to the paralysed man, 'Son, your sins are forgiven.'

Now some teachers of the law were sitting there, thinking to themselves, 'Why does this fellow talk like that? He's blaspheming! Who can forgive sins but God alone?'

Immediately Jesus knew in his spirit that this was what they were thinking in their hearts, and he said to them, 'Why are you thinking these things? Which is easier: to say to this paralysed man, "Your sins are forgiven", or to say, "Get up, take your mat and walk"? But I want you to know that the Son of Man has authority on earth to forgive sins.' So he said to the man, 'I tell you, get up, take your mat and go home.' He got up, took his mat and walked out in full view of them all. This amazed everyone and they praised God, saying, 'We have never seen anything like this!'

Mark 2:1–12

In the time of Jesus, illness was often thought to be the result of sin. Some Jews thought in terms of punishment; others made a psychological connection between illness and sin, believing that guilt may have physical consequences. This seems to have been the case with this man's paralysis, as Jesus said, 'Your sins are forgiven', rather than, 'You are cured'. The scribes were scandalised, as it was blasphemous to claim an authority to forgive sins that belonged only to God. Jesus replied that because he was the Son of Man, he was God's

Objectives

Explore the ways in which Jesus referred to himself as the Son of Man.

Consider the importance of the title Son of Man for 21st-century Christians.

A *The remains of houses in Capernaum, the village where Jesus healed the paralysed man*

Activity

1 Work in groups of five. Each person should take one of the following roles: the formerly paralysed man; one of his friends; one of the crowd; and a scribe who was there. The fifth person should be a journalist, interviewing the others. Prepare and perform a role play to represent the views described above about the nature of illness and the authority to forgive sins.

Extension activity

Read Mark 2:23–28. This is not a set passage for study, but it shows the other occasion when Jesus referred to his authority as Son of Man in a conflict situation. The incident concerned the use of the Sabbath day. What do you think Jesus meant when he said: 'So the Son of Man is Lord even of the Sabbath'?

representative and acted with God's authority. Therefore, he had the right to declare that the man's sins were forgiven. He then proved this authority by telling the man to get up, which he did.

Jesus' suffering

Jesus often used the title Son of Man when talking about his suffering, for example at Caesarea Philippi. It showed his vulnerability as a human being who would be rejected, suffer and die. He was also influenced by some poems in the book of Isaiah about a humble 'suffering servant'. He told his disciples that the Son of Man had come as a servant, who would give his life for humanity.

∞ links

For Caesarea Philippi read pages 42–45; for the Suffering Servant poems, Isaiah 50:6; 53:1–12; for Jesus' teaching on service, see pages 132–133.

Jesus' future glory

On several occasions Jesus said that his death was not the end; God would raise him to glory. During his trial before the Sanhedrin, Jesus stated that he was the Messiah. He then went on to say that they would see the Son of Man seated at God's right hand and coming on the clouds of heaven.

C *Jesus the Son of Man coming on the clouds of heaven*

B *The crucifixion showed Jesus at his most vulnerable*

∞ links

Read pages 58–59 for Jesus' trial before the Sanhedrin.

This title's importance for 21st-century Christians

Many Christians find this title attractive. It emphasises Jesus' humanity and his humility. At the same time, it points to his authority as God's representative during his ministry and to his future state of glory. It reminds them of the good news that Jesus came as saviour and shows his selfless love, as he lived to serve others and was then prepared to die for them. It was also the title preferred by Jesus. Some Christians, however, find it hard to relate to a Jewish title so tied to the Old Testament and the 1st century. It can also seem vague.

Study tip

The title Son of Man has a number of meanings. It is important that you know what these are and understand how they relate to the life and death of Jesus. Do not confuse this title with Son of God.

Activity

2 Read through all the pages on the Son of Man. Then write four headings: 'The title Jesus preferred for himself'; 'Jesus the suffering Son of Man'; 'Jesus the humble servant'; 'Jesus the authoritative Son of Man'. Write at least two sentences showing how each of the headings is illustrated in Mark's Gospel. If you completed the activity on page 87, you will find that information useful here.

Summary

You should now know how Jesus applied the title Son of Man to himself and understand differing views on its importance in helping Christians today to understand the Person of Jesus.

Introduction: the Jewish background

The term **Son of God** was used for three groups of people in the Old Testament. Mostly it referred to the nation of Israel. It conveyed the intimate relationship that existed between God and his chosen people. It was also used of Old Testament kings, who were declared at their coronations to be God's adopted sons. This indicated a very special relationship between God and the king and the king's role as a representative of Israel. Faithful Jews were called sons of God. They were seen as the true people of God.

Jesus as Son of God

Jesus did not call himself the Son of God, but it was a title that Mark saw as particularly important. For him, as for his readers, Jesus' relationship with God was unique. He was not an adopted son of God or a son of God in the sense of a faithful Jew, but the Son of God by nature. Mark believed that Jesus was like God in a unique sense. The title occurs at significant points in Mark's Gospel (see the Links):

- as Mark's introduction to the Gospel
- at the key events of the baptism and transfiguration
- as the key question at the trial before the Sanhedrin
- immediately after Jesus died.

Mark might have intended his readers to see a connection between the last two references. At his trial, the supreme representative of the Jews, Caiaphas, asked Jesus if he was the Son of the Blessed One (i.e. of God). Caiaphas clearly did not believe this to be true. Jesus replied that he was. The title was used again after Jesus' death in the declaration by a Gentile that Jesus was, indeed, the Son of God. Whatever the centurion meant, for Mark it was a declaration of faith.

A *Occasions when Jesus was called Son of God*

Reference and words	Speaker	Context
1:1: The beginning of the gospel about Jesus Christ, the Son of God.	Mark	Introduction to the gospel
1:11: 'You are my Son, whom I love, with you I am well pleased.'	God	Jesus' baptism
3:11: 'You are the Son of God.'	Demon-possessed people	People came for healing
9:7: 'This is my Son, whom I love. Listen to him!'	God	Jesus' transfiguration
14:61 'Are you the Christ, the Son of the Blessed One?'	The high priest	The trial before the Sanhedrin
15:39: 'Surely this man was the Son of God!'	The centurion	Jesus' crucifixion

Objectives

Know how the title Son of God was used in the Old Testament and to understand its meaning for Mark and his readers.

Explore reasons for it giving special insight into the Person of Jesus.

Key terms

Son of God: a title used for Jesus; Christians believe that before his birth as a human being, Jesus had always existed as God the Son. Also as used by the centurion after Jesus' death; means 'a Righteous Man'.

Beliefs and teachings

'Israel is my firstborn son …'

Exodus 4:22

Beliefs and teachings

'You are my Son;
Today I have become your Father.'

Psalms 2:7

links

Read about when Mark uses this title: introduction to the Gospel, pages 8–9; baptism and transfiguration, pages 38–39, pages 46–47; trial before the Sanhedrin, pages 58–59; the crucifixion, pages 62–67.

Jesus was also declared to be Son of God by demon-possessed people. It was believed in the ancient world that demons had supernatural knowledge. Although they were forces of evil, Mark believed that they recognised the true nature of Jesus' relationship with God.

Activities

1 Why was Israel sometimes referred to as the Son of God?

2 In what way was Mark's belief about Jesus being the Son of God different from the Jewish understanding of kings as sons of God?

3 What might the centurion have meant when he said that Jesus was the Son of God? (If you are not sure, read pages 64–65 again.)

◼ The baptism of Jesus (Mark 1:9–11)

∞ links

Read this set text and the explanation of it on pages 38–39 before working through this section.

According to Mark's Gospel, Jesus was very aware of his unique relationship with God and of the mission to which God had called him. As Son of God, he fulfilled the role and relationship with God that Israel and Israel's former kings were meant to have, and so God was pleased with him. But it went further than that. Mark wrote his gospel in Greek, and the Greek word translated here as 'whom I love' or 'beloved' is sometimes used in a special sense to mean 'only'. Many scholars think that in Mark's account of Jesus' baptism (and also in the transfiguration), Jesus was addressed as 'my only Son'.

◼ The importance of this title for 21st-century Christians

Many Christians think that this is the best title for Jesus as it states clearly what Christianity teaches. It is not vague, it has no political links, and nor is it tied to a particular culture. Christians, whatever their nationality, can understand it. It shows the closeness of Jesus' relationship with God and it reminds them of his power to heal and to save. Some Christians, however, find it off-putting. Although they accept it as part of Christian belief, they prefer to think of Jesus as a more personal figure to whom they can be close. The Son of God can seem more remote.

B   *The baptism of Jesus*

Study tip

Exam questions might be set on whether or not particular titles help modern Christians to understand the Person of Jesus. Ensure that you are prepared for such a question.

Discussion activity

Divide into three groups. Each group should be allocated one of the three titles for Jesus studied in this chapter (Christ/Messiah, Son of Man and Son of God). The task is to prepare and then present to the rest of the class a case for that title giving the best insight into the Person of Jesus in the 21st century. The group should discuss the title and what it might mean to modern Christians before putting together their presentation. At the end of the presentations, there should be a whole-class discussion about the three titles. Which title/s does the class prefer, and why?

Summary

By now you should know the Jewish background to the title Son of God and understand its significance for Mark and his readers. You should also be able to evaluate its relevance for 21st-century Christians.

The Person of Jesus – summary

For the examination, you should now be able to:

✔ understand the Person of Jesus as teacher and miracle worker, with particular reference to the feeding of the five thousand

✔ know and understand the background to the following titles of Jesus

    – Christ/Messiah

    – Son of Man

    – Son of God

✔ understand the insights these titles give into the Person of Jesus, and their significance for Christians today

✔ know and understand the following set texts

    – the feeding of the five thousand (Mark 6:30–44)

    – the baptism of Jesus (Mark 1:9–11)

    – the paralysed man (Mark 2:1–12)

    – Caesarea Philippi (Mark 8:27–33).

Sample answer

1 Write an answer to the following exam question:

Explain how Jesus used the title 'Son of Man'. You should refer to Mark's Gospel in your answer. *(6 marks)*

2 a Read the following sample answer:

> Jesus used the title Son of Man in three different ways. It was his favourite title for himself. He used it to show his authority, e.g. to forgive sins and to ignore Sabbath law. He used it whenever he predicted his suffering and death, and he used it to refer to his future glory.

  b With a partner, discuss the sample answer. The answer refers in some detail to one of the ways, but just lists the other two ways. What extra detail do you think might have been included? Do you think that there are other things that the student could have included in the answer?

  c What mark would you give this answer out of 6? Look at the mark scheme in the Introduction on page 7 (AO1). What are the reasons for the mark you have given?

Practice questions

1 What does the word 'Messiah' mean? *(1 mark)*

2 Why did Jesus not want to be called Messiah? *(2 marks)*

3 'Jesus was more important as a teacher than as a miracle worker.'
What do you think? Give your opinion. *(3 marks)*

4 Describe the healing of the paralysed man. *(6 marks)*

Study tip For evaluation questions marked out of 3 you should simply state and justify what you think on a religious issue, not give alternative viewpoints. You will, therefore, not need to write as much as if there were 6 marks available.

5.1 The Sabbath in the time of Jesus

■ The Sabbath

According to the Old Testament, after escaping from Egypt Moses led the Israelites through the wilderness to Mount Sinai. There he received the Ten Commandments from God. One of these is concerned with the Sabbath, the Jewish holy day, which lasts from Friday dusk until Saturday dusk each week.

The Commandment relating to the Sabbath

A *Michelangelo's sculpture of Moses*

> **Beliefs and teachings**
>
> Remember the Sabbath day by keeping it holy. Six days you shall labour and do all your work, but the seventh day is a Sabbath to the Lord your God. On it you shall not do any work …
>
> *Exodus 20:8–10*

The Hebrew word *shabbat* means 'to rest', and the Sabbath was to be a day of total rest for the whole community. This included slaves and work animals; it originally included non-Jews who were resident in Israel, though by the time of Jesus this would not have been the case. The Old Testament gave two reasons for this day of rest.

Firstly, it was linked to the story about the creation of the world, where it was said that God completed his work in six days and rested on the seventh. God, therefore, made the seventh day different from the working week.

> **Beliefs and teachings**
>
> And God blessed the seventh day and made it holy, because on it he rested from all the work of creating that he had done.
>
> *Genesis 2:3*

Secondly, in the Old Testament book Deuteronomy, which also listed the Ten Commandments, observing the Sabbath was linked to the escape of the Jews from Egypt. The inclusion of servants in the rest day was a reminder that those Jews who escaped had been slaves.

> **Beliefs and teachings**
>
> Observe the Sabbath day by keeping it holy … On it you shall not do any work, neither you … nor your manservant or maidservant, … so that your manservant and maidservant may rest, as you do. Remember that you were slaves in Egypt and that the Lord your God brought you out of there with a mighty hand … Therefore the Lord your God has commanded you to observe the Sabbath day.
>
> *Deuteronomy 5:12, 14–15*

> **Objectives**
>
> Study the Commandment, the oral tradition and the reasons given for celebrating the Sabbath.
>
> Understand Jesus' disputes with the authorities over this issue.

> **Discussion activity** 👥👥👥
>
> Many people, not just Jews, think that having a regular rest day is a good idea, promoting physical, mental and spiritual health. Discuss in small groups or pairs what you think about this and about the reasons given in the Old Testament for a day of rest.

The scribes' oral tradition

The **Sabbath** was intended to be a day of joyful celebration. In the 1st century, as now, it was observed in the synagogue and in the home. Jewish men went to the synagogue services on Friday and Saturday. It was also a time for being at home with the family, enjoying the Sabbath meal that had been prepared earlier on the Friday and studying the Torah together. The day was seen as God's gift to his chosen people. Moreover, the Jews believed that if every Jew obeyed all the Torah's commands, the Kingdom of God would come. It was therefore important that ordinary Jews should understand exactly what they were allowed to do. This would enable them to enjoy the gift of the Sabbath to the full and also to feel that they were playing their part in keeping the Law.

It was for this reason that the scribes explained precisely what 'work' on the Sabbath meant as part of the oral tradition. This was a kind of commentary on the written Torah; it was intended to be helpful and was described as forming a fence around the Law. It protected the holiness of the Torah. As part of this oral tradition there were 39 Sabbath prohibitions – things Jews were not allowed to do on the Sabbath.

Key terms

Sabbath: the Jewish day of rest, from sunset on Friday to sunset on Saturday.

Study tip

You might think that keeping the Sabbath laws would be difficult. Try to understand the Jewish view of the Sabbath as a gift from God, to help you to explain Jesus' conflict with the authorities and to evaluate his actions.

 Welcoming in the Sabbath at home

Research activity

The Sabbath

Go to the website listed in the Links opposite. Click on Shabbat and then on 39. Print off or write out a list of the Sabbath prohibitions. It will be useful to have these to refer to when you study, in the next pages, how Jesus ignored them. If you cannot access this site, try researching the Sabbath prohibitions using a search engine.

∞ **links**

Use the following website to help with the Research activity: www.akhlah.com.

Summary

You should now know and understand the reasons for observing the Sabbath as a background to understanding the disputes on this issue between Jesus and the authorities.

5.2 Jesus and the Jewish authorities: the Sabbath

The man with the withered hand (Mark 3:1–6)

Beliefs and teachings

Another time he went into the synagogue, and a man with a shrivelled hand was there. Some of them were looking for a reason to accuse Jesus, so they watched him closely to see if he would heal him on the Sabbath. Jesus said to the man with the shrivelled hand, 'Stand up in front of everyone.' Then Jesus asked them, 'Which is lawful on the Sabbath: to do good or to do evil, to save life or to kill?' But they remained silent. He looked round at them in anger and, deeply distressed at their stubborn hearts, said to the man, 'Stretch out your hand.' He stretched it out, and his hand was completely restored. Then the Pharisees went out and began to plot with the Herodians how they might kill Jesus.

Mark 3:1–6

Activity

1 Read again through Mark's account of the healing of the man with the withered hand in the Beliefs and teachings box. Then, from memory, write out the story in your own words. Check your account against the set text and make sure you have included all the key facts.

Several times in Mark's Gospel, Jesus was recorded as attending the synagogue on the Sabbath. The religious leaders opposed to Jesus might have ensured the disabled man was placed there so that Jesus could not miss seeing him. According to the Old Testament, death was the penalty for breaking the Sabbath law, although it is unlikely that this could have been carried out in the 1st century. Nevertheless, such an accusation could have damaged Jesus' reputation and authority as a teacher.

The oral tradition counted healing as work, though in an emergency, saving life came before keeping the Sabbath law. This man's disability, however, was not a life-threatening one, and his healing could have waited. However, Jesus tried to make the Pharisees think at a deeper level than the Law. The Torah was intended to give glory to God and to help humans. Saving life was more than just an action to prevent death; it was about enabling someone to enjoy life to the full, emotionally and spiritually as well as physically. Surely then, in healing this man, Jesus was fulfilling the Torah?

The religious leaders' refusal to rethink their position both angered and grieved Jesus, but the man had no doubts. He obeyed Jesus' command and his hand was cured. Jesus could not be accused of disobeying the Law, as he healed him by word only; this was not an offence. The hatred that the Pharisees felt for Jesus was shown in their alliance with men whose views they despised, the Herodians. Jesus was now seen as a threat by both religious and secular authorities.

Objectives

Study Mark's account of Jesus healing the man with the withered (paralysed) hand.

Understand why Jesus disagreed with the Pharisees about the use of the Sabbath.

links

Read about the Pharisees and Herodians on pages 32–33.

links

Read the story of the paralysed man on pages 88–89 to reinforce your understanding of these as two different stories.

A *Ruins of an ancient synagogue in Capernaum, like the one where Jesus healed the man on the Sabbath*

Activities

2 Read Mark 2:23–28. This is not a set passage for study, but it relates another incident when Jesus came into conflict with Pharisees over Sabbath observance. When you have read the text, work through these questions.

a What rules were Jesus' disciples breaking on this occasion? (If you are unsure of the answer, look again at the website listed on page 95, or the notes you made for the Research activity, if you completed this.)

b Why do you think Jesus chose an example of David breaking the Law to defend what he did? (Again, if you are unsure of the answer, read about David on pages 50–51 and 82–83.)

c Explain in your own words what you think Jesus meant by the Sabbath being made for man, not man for the Sabbath.

Beliefs and teachings

The Sabbath was made for man, not man for the Sabbath. So the Son of man is Lord even of the Sabbath.

Mark 2:27–28

∞ links

Use this website to help with the discussion activity:
www.lordsday.co.uk

Discussion activity

1 a If you discussed the Sabbath when studying pages 94–95, review your ideas and conclusions. Then, in small groups, read through what is written here.

For Christians, Sunday is a holy day. Some believe no work other than what is essential, such as cooking, should be done on that day.

You could find out more about that viewpoint by going to the website suggested in the Links.

Some see Sunday as a good day, for going to church, being with family and doing something to help others, e.g. visiting a lonely person.

Other Christians believe that as long as they attend church, the rest of the day is for them to use as they wish, e.g. shopping.

b Which of these Christian views do you think is the closest to Jesus' own view of the Sabbath? If there is disagreement in the group, that does not matter. Most Christians would say that there is no right answer to this; it is a matter of interpretation.

B *How do you think Christians should spend Sunday – praying, shopping, visiting?*

Summary

You should now know the story of the man with the withered hand and understand how and why Jesus disagreed with the Pharisees regarding the Sabbath on this occasion.

Study tip

Do not confuse Jesus' healing of the paralysed man with his healing of the man with the withered (paralysed) hand. Conflict in the first story was about forgiveness; in the second it was about the Sabbath rules.

Jesus and the Jewish authorities: the Temple Court

The Temple Court

The Temple Court, also known as the Court of the Gentiles, was the huge outer area of the Temple complex. The Sanhedrin hired it out for the selling of animals and birds for sacrifice. (These had to be without any blemish, as only the best was good enough for God, so worshippers could not just bring their own animals.) Pilgrims to Jerusalem were required to pay an annual half-shekel Temple tax. The Temple Court was the area where the pilgrims could change their Roman coins into the special coinage needed for this tax.

The Court of the Gentiles was meant to be a place for Gentiles to worship God. It was the only place available for this in the Temple. It was separated from the rest of the Temple by a barrier with notices warning that Gentiles who went beyond would be killed. Yet with all the bustle of the selling of animals and conversion of currency, praying there must have been like trying to pray in the middle of a busy supermarket on Christmas Eve.

Jesus in the Temple Court (Mark 11:15–18)

Beliefs and teachings

On reaching Jerusalem, Jesus entered the temple area and began driving out those who were buying and selling there. He overturned the tables of the moneychangers and the benches of those selling doves, and would not allow anyone to carry merchandise through the temple courts. And as he taught them, he said, 'Is it not written: "My house will be called a house of prayer for all nations"? But you have made it a "den of robbers".' The chief priests and the teachers of the law heard this and began looking for a way to kill him, for they feared him, because the whole crowd was amazed at his teaching.

Mark 11:15–18

Jesus' actions in the Temple Court were very dramatic, but it could have been no more than a relatively small-scale, symbolic protest. He could not possibly have cleared the court of all merchants, and they would in any case have returned as soon as he left. Nevertheless, it was a bold thing to do. Jesus was challenging the authority of the Sanhedrin. He was, in a sense, signing his own death warrant, as the religious authorities could not ignore this incident. He was probably making a protest against the hypocrisy of the religious leaders. The Temple was intended to be a place where Gentiles as well as Jews could worship God. This was impossible because of the trading and money changing, which also brought in a huge profit for the Sanhedrin.

Discussion activity 👥

1 In pairs, discuss Jesus' protest in the Temple. Given that it did not change anything, do you think there was any point in what he did? Do you think he was right to use violence, or do you think his anger got the better of him?

Objectives

Study Jesus' protest in the Temple Court and explore possible reasons for his action.

Consider whether violent protest is ever justified.

🔗 links

Read about the Temple on pages 34–35.

A *A half-shekel like the ones used to pay taxes*

B *Praying at the Wailing Wall – the one remaining part of the 1st-century Temple*

Christian attitudes to protest

Jesus' anger at the misuse of the Court of the Gentiles led to him using violence. There is no indication that he assaulted anyone, but he must have used force to drive them out and turn over the tables. Some Christians find this story very difficult to understand. They are totally opposed to any use of violence, whatever the situation, as they believe it achieves nothing in the longer term. They support only **non-violent protest**. Other Christians claim that Jesus' action was justified; it was the response of righteous anger to something that was wrong. In certain situations they would accept limited violent protest as long as it did not actually hurt anyone. Sometimes, they argue, this is the only way people will take note of the protest and put things right.

Key terms

Non-violent protest: a demonstration or other action which draws attention to wrong without resorting to violence.

Case study

Environmental protest

In 2007 five members of Greenpeace climbed the huge tower of a coal-fired power station. They caused £30,000 of damage. Although they were prepared to pay the estimated costs of repair, the prosecutor claimed that they had gone beyond the acceptable limits of protest. The Greenpeace activists claimed that their aim was to prevent the loss of life and further damage to property that would result from global warming, caused in part by such power stations.

Discussion activities

2 Discuss in small groups what you think about the Greenpeace protest explained in the case study above. If you think their action was justified, would your decision have been different if they had not declared their willingness to pay the repairs bill?

3 Now discuss if, or when, violence is ever justified in a protest. Do you think that non-violent protest is more effective than the use of violence? You may wish to use the images of different kinds of protest to give you ideas. Give your reasons for your opinions.

Research activity

Use a search engine to find out more about people who have used non-violent protest, for example Martin Luther King.

C   *What kind of protest is the most effective?*

Study tip

You must be able to state your opinion on the issue of violent and non-violent protest. Do you think violent protest is always wrong or can it sometimes be justified? If the latter, are there limits to what is acceptable?

Summary

You should now understand the reasons for Jesus' protest in the Court of the Gentiles. You should also have considered whether or not his protest was effective and whether violent protests are ever justified.

5.4 Jesus and the Jewish authorities: paying Roman taxes

▮ Roman taxation

All their conquered peoples had to pay annual taxes to the Romans. Tax was imposed on Judaea in 6 CE when it came under direct Roman rule with a Roman governor. The Jews bitterly resented the taxation. When it was first introduced, there was a major rebellion and the Zealot movement was born. This resentment was expressed throughout the 1st century. It was one of the causes of the Jewish War in 66 CE that resulted, four years later, in the destruction of Jerusalem. So, during the lifetime of Jesus the question of paying tax to the Romans was a burning issue.

Objectives

Study Mark's account of the debate over payment of taxes to Caesar.

Explore the meaning of Jesus' reply for his audience and for 1st-century Christians

Beliefs and teachings

Later they sent some of the Pharisees and Herodians to Jesus to catch him in his words. They came to him and said, 'Teacher, we know you are a man of integrity. You aren't swayed by men, because you pay no attention to who they are; but you teach the way of God in accordance with the truth. Is it right to pay taxes to Caesar or not? Should we pay or shouldn't we?' But Jesus knew their hypocrisy. 'Why are you trying to trap me?' he asked. 'Bring me a denarius and let me look at it.' They brought the coin, and he asked them, 'Whose portrait is this? And whose inscription?' 'Caesar's,' they replied. Then Jesus said to them, 'Give to Caesar what is Caesar's and to God what is God's.' And they were amazed at him.

Mark 12:13–17

A *Part of the arch of Titus in Rome, celebrating the destruction of Jerusalem and the Temple in 70 CE*

⬭links

To read about how Judaea became a Roman province, see pages 30–31; and about the Zealots, pages 32–33.

▮ Payment of taxes to Caesar (Mark 12:13–17)

As in the story of the healing of the man with the withered hand, there is in this incident a surprising alliance of Pharisees and Herodians. Both would probably have supported (though reluctantly) the payment of the Roman tax. The Pharisees were opposed to open rebellion, and supporters of the Herod family had to accept Roman authority to keep their status. Jesus saw through their flattery and would have known he must reply carefully. If he opposed payment of the tax, then he would have been reported to the Romans as a threat to state security, and arrested. If he supported the tax, he would have lost the support of ordinary Jews who resented it. This would have undermined his authority and popularity and made it easier for the religious authorities to get rid of him before he was ready.

So Jesus asked for the silver coin which was used for the tax. Coins bearing the image of the Roman Emperor broke one of the Ten Commandments (see the Beliefs and teachings box), so were offensive to Jews. Nevertheless, one of his critics had one of the coins. This, in itself, implied acceptance of the authority of Rome. Jesus' final statement was very clever. The Jews had a duty both to the state and to God, but he left the decision on how to apply this to those listening.

Beliefs and teachings

Everyone must submit himself to the governing authorities … Give everyone what you owe him: If you owe taxes, pay taxes; if revenue, then revenue; if respect, then respect; if honour, then honour.

Romans 13:1, 7

⬭links

Read about the Pharisees and Herodians on pages 32–33.

1   Why do you think the Jews hated paying the annual tax?

2   Explain why the question about payment of taxes was a tricky one for Jesus to answer.

3   Jesus asked one of his critics for a denarius, which would bear the head of the emperor. Why do you think he did this?

4   What was Jesus implying in his teaching: 'Give to Caesar what is Caesar's and to God what is God's'?

You shall not make for yourself an idol in the form of anything in heaven above or on the earth beneath or in the waters below.

Exodus 20:4

The importance of this story for 1st-century Christians

Mark's Gospel was written either during the Jewish War or just after the Roman legions captured Jerusalem and destroyed the Temple. Although this war was limited to Jews in Palestine, it was a difficult time for Jews and Jewish Christians in the rest of the Roman Empire. Added to that, Christians (of both Jewish and Gentile backgrounds) were, themselves, facing or had recently faced persecution. Their refusal to worship the Emperor Nero as a god was seen as rebellion. Jesus' teaching on the payment of taxation applied to the question of obedience to state authorities. Christians believed that they were members of the Kingdom of God. Did this mean that they should ignore the demands of the state, even if it meant death? Christian teachers reaffirmed Jesus' teaching: Christians had duties both to the state and to God and should be good and obedient citizens. Paul had written on this topic to Christians in Rome only ten years before Mark wrote his gospel (see the Beliefs and teachings box).

B   *Replica denarius showing the image of the Emperor Nero*

1   Read through these pages again and then divide into small groups to discuss the following questions. You might find it helpful to read the background information about the persecution of Christians (see Links below).

a   How might those Christians who were facing persecution in Rome have applied the teaching of Jesus and Paul to their everyday lives?

b   If you had been one of those Christians, how far would you have made compromises to live in peace and avoid persecution?

c   At what point, if any, would you have been prepared to disobey the demands of the emperor?

⊂⊃ links

You can read about the persecution of Christians in Rome on pages 22–23.

You should now know Mark's account of the debate about paying Roman taxes and understand Jesus' reply to the Pharisees' questions. You should understand the difficulties for Christians in knowing when obeying God should come before obeying the state.

Remember that Mark's Gospel was written to encourage Christians living in difficult circumstances in Rome. When you study incidents like the one on these pages, think about their meaning for those early Christians as well as modern Christianity.

Introduction

Jesus came into conflict with the authorities over a number of issues: forgiveness of sins; allowing his disciples to break Sabbath law, and breaking it himself by healing; the misuse of the Court of the Gentiles; the question of paying tax; and befriending outcasts. He was hated by both religious and secular leaders and his views and actions resulted in his arrest and death.

∞ links

Read about Jesus' conflict with the authorities on pages 96–101; and about his attitude to the outcast on pages 104–109.

Christian attitudes to authority

The New Testament teaches Christians to respect religious and **secular** authorities. It says that they should be respected and obeyed as their authority to rule comes from God. Christians take this teaching seriously, but there have been occasions when some have felt it was right to defy the authorities, whatever the consequences.

Objectives

Explore Christian attitudes to authority.

Consider why Christians have sometimes been prepared to disobey the government, even if it meant imprisonment or death.

Key terms

Secular: a set of beliefs which does not need to have God or religion in them.

Discussion activities

Work through the following questions as a whole-class discussion.

1. If the government passed laws allowing something you thought was very wrong, or made laws that infringed civil liberties, would you be prepared to make a stand?

2. How far would you be willing to go in opposing the government? Would you, for example, write letters of complaint, or would you go further and break the law?

3. Is there any principle for which you would be willing to go to prison?

∞ links

Re-read the case study of James Mawdsley on page 27 for an example of a Christian defying a secular authority.

Religious authorities

In the Church of England, the General Synod (the decision-making body) voted in 1994 to allow women to be made priests. This was supported by the Archbishop of Canterbury, who is the most important leader in the Church of England. Not everyone agreed with this decision. Arrangements were made so that those who disagreed could remain part of the Church of England without having to recognise the ordination of women. Many, however, felt so strongly that they left the Church of England. They were not prepared to compromise and, instead, challenged the authority of their religious leaders.

A *Some Christians do not recognise women priests*

Secular authorities

Opposing the government can be costly. In the UK, if it involves breaking the law, it can lead to imprisonment. In the late 20th century a poll tax was introduced by the British government. This worked on similar lines to 1st-century Roman taxation. Every adult British citizen above a certain income level had to pay the same sum regardless of their level of wealth. Some Christians felt that this was very wrong. They thought it was unjust that people on lower incomes had to pay the same amount as those earning high salaries. They, therefore, refused to pay the tax on principle, which they stuck to even when taken to court. Some were put in prison for non-payment.

In some countries, those who oppose the government are killed. In the last hundred years or so there have been many Christian martyrs, killed by their rulers because of their protests against discrimination, injustice and corruption. Ten of these are commemorated on the West Front of Westminster Abbey.

links

For more about discrimination, see pages 104–109.

Case study

Dietrich Bonhoeffer

Dietrich Bonhoeffer was a Christian minister in Germany at the time when Hitler and his Nazi supporters ruled Germany. Many Christians accepted their policies, but Bonhoeffer believed that they were evil. He had been a pacifist and had always taken seriously New Testament teachings about respecting civil authorities, but in this situation he believed that to be truly Christian, he must disobey Hitler and his government. He helped Jews escape arrest and he became increasingly involved in movements that were plotting the overthrow of the Nazis. In 1943 he was arrested and put in prison. A year later a plot to assassinate Hitler was discovered. It failed but hundreds of political prisoners were executed as a result. In April 1945, less than a month before the end of the Second World War, Bonhoeffer was executed.

B　*20th-century Christian martyrs on the West Front of Westminster Abbey*

Research activity

The West Front martyrs

Using the Westminster Abbey website or a search engine, make a list of the ten martyrs commemorated on the West Front. Choose one or more of these martyrs and find out more about them. Make notes on each. You might have studied Oscar Romero in Chapter 1 – if so, refer back to your notes. You can also use the case study above for information on Dietrich Bonhoeffer.

links

Use the following link for the activities:

www.westminster-abbey.org. Type 'Ten modern martyrs' into the search box then click on The nave and you will find them listed in the final paragraph, headed 'the West Window'.

Extension activity

These ten modern martyrs come from very different backgrounds. Choose any three of them and note what they have in common.

Study tip

You need to understand why some Christians have felt it necessary to disobey religious and/or state authorities. Knowing about specific examples of such Christians might make this easier for you to understand and remember.

Summary

You should now understand why Christians might disobey religious and/or secular authorities, and you should know about some examples of individual Christians who did this.

5.6　Jesus and the outcast (1)

■ Introduction

There were many different groups of people who were treated as **outcasts** or looked down on in 1st-century Jewish society. Some Jews were despised because they did not keep all the rules found in the written and oral Law. Others were shunned because they worked for the hated Romans. Those with certain illnesses were excluded from society, and men who were disabled were not allowed into the men's part of the Temple. All Jewish women were denied the same rights as men, and were regarded as inferior. Foreigners were avoided as much as possible.

Tax collectors were another group of outcasts. The Jews not only had to pay the poll tax to Rome, they were also taxed on their produce, for example, fish if they were fishermen. The Romans employed people to collect these taxes on their behalf, so tax collectors were seen as traitors to the Jewish cause. Ordinary Jews also hated them as they were known to be dishonest, collecting more than the set amount in order to make an extra income for themselves. Strict Jews despised them because they deliberately ignored the Law's requirements.

Mark related a number of incidents in which Jesus accepted outcasts, showing them love and compassion. Mark intended his writing to be seen as good news, which is very clear in these stories, examined below.

⬭⬭ links

Read the pages that follow about outcasts; also about the status of women on pages 52–53 and pages 64–65.

■ The call of Levi (Mark 2:13–14)

> **Beliefs and teachings**
>
> Once again Jesus went out beside the lake. A large crowd came to him, and he began to teach them. As he walked along, he saw Levi son of Alphaeus sitting at the tax collector's booth. 'Follow me,' Jesus told him, and Levi got up and followed him.
>
> *Mark 2:13–14*

It might have amazed people that Jesus' first disciples were humble fishermen. But choosing a tax collector must really have shocked the crowd, including those disciples whom he had already chosen. The four fishermen had probably been cheated in the past by Levi, whose response to Jesus' call was immediate. Levi (known elsewhere in the New Testament as Matthew) left a job that earned him a great deal of money to follow a wandering preacher.

⬭⬭ links

Read about Jesus calling the fishermen on pages 118–119.

> **Objectives**
>
> Consider which groups were looked down on by 1st-century Jews and the reasons for this.
>
> Study the call of Levi and the meal at his house, and explore Jesus' understanding of his mission.

> **Key terms**
>
> **Outcasts:** those who were rejected by others in society, e.g. lepers, and not given fair treatment.

A *Tax collectors were despised by most 1st-century Jews*

Eating with sinners (Mark 2:15–17)

Beliefs and teachings

While Jesus was having dinner at Levi's house, many tax collectors and 'sinners' were eating with him and his disciples, for there were many who followed him. When the teachers of the Law who were Pharisees saw him eating with the 'sinners' and tax collectors, they asked his disciples, 'Why does he eat with tax collectors and "sinners"?' On hearing this, Jesus said to them, 'It is not the healthy who need a doctor, but the sick. I have not come to call the righteous, but sinners.'

Mark 2:15–17

B   *Statue of Matthew the tax collector*

By entering the house of a tax collector, a sinner, Jesus made himself ritually unclean according to the Jewish Law. This would have been made worse when he ate there. The food laws were very complicated but central to Jewish faith. The food he ate would not have been properly prepared, and he might have touched dishes that were considered unclean. By 'sinners' Mark probably meant those who quite deliberately broke or ignored the Law.

It is not surprising that the Pharisees were scandalised: Jesus claimed to be carrying out God's work, yet did not seem concerned that Levi and his dinner guests had no intention of observing God's Law. Jesus' reply showed a totally different understanding of his mission. In the same way that a doctor helps the physically ill, he was there to cure the spiritually sick. Far from being contaminated by mixing with sinners, he brought forgiveness and hope to those whom everyone else hated.

Activity

1   Read through the set text and these pages again. Then answer the following questions. When you have finished, check your answers for accuracy.

   a   Give three reasons why tax collectors were hated so much by other Jews.

   b   Why do you think Jesus' choice of a tax collector as a disciple would have been more surprising than his choice of fishermen?

   c   Why was the idea of Jesus eating with Levi and his friends so offensive to the Pharisees?

Discussion activity

1   a   Divide into groups of five. Discuss first of all what you think might have made Jesus choose a tax collector as a disciple. What potential might he have seen in Levi?

   b   Prepare a role play. Four of the group should be the four fishermen (Simon Peter, Andrew, James and John) whom Jesus had already called to be disciples. If it would help, read the account of their call in Mark 1:16–20. The fifth person should be Levi. Imagine that the meal at Levi's house has ended and the five of you are left alone together. Make up the kind of conversation that you might have had. Bear in mind the fact that the fishermen had probably been overcharged by Levi many times in the past, but also consider how they might have been influenced by Jesus' teaching at the meal.

   c   Present your role plays to the rest of the class and discuss as a class the ideas that you have all come up with.

Study tip

As well as showing Jesus' attitude to outcasts, the story of the meal at Levi's house shows Jesus in conflict with the Pharisees. It would be another example to give in a question about Jesus' relationship with the Jewish authorities.

Summary

You should now know the set text about the call of Levi and what followed, as well as understanding both why tax collectors were despised and how this story demonstrates how Jesus saw his mission.

5.7 Jesus and the outcast (2)

Leprosy

Leprosy is an illness that still creates fear and despair among the people living in those countries where it is common. If untreated, it can be disfiguring and disabling, and people can die as a result of complications caused by the disease. Those who develop it might be driven out of their homes and villages.

In 1st-century Israel, sufferers were always excluded, as the disease was thought to be passed on by contact. Those with leprosy were thought to be unclean. The Old Testament gave detailed instructions for diagnosing leprosy, excluding the sufferer and checking that those who claimed to be cured did, in fact, no longer have the disease. Several other skin diseases were thought to be leprosy, so occasionally people did seem to recover, though it was rare. There was a saying of the rabbis that curing a person with leprosy was as hard as raising the dead.

The man with leprosy (Mark 1:40–44)

> ### Beliefs and teachings
>
> A man with leprosy came to him and begged him on his knees, 'If you are willing, you can make me clean.' Filled with compassion, Jesus reached out his hand and touched the man. 'I am willing,' he said. 'Be clean!' Immediately the leprosy left him and he was cured. Jesus sent him away at once with a strong warning: 'See that you don't tell this to anyone. But go, show yourself to the priest and offer the sacrifices that Moses commanded for your cleansing, as a testimony to them.'
>
> *Mark 1:40–44*

Under the rules for someone with leprosy, the man should not have approached Jesus, but his desperation can be seen in the way he fell on his knees and begged for help. He had faith in Jesus' ability to cure him but, as he was an outcast, he could not be sure that Jesus would be willing to heal him. Jesus often used touch in healing, but in this situation it was a surprising action. Not only did those at the time believe he ran the risk of contracting the disease, but physical contact also contaminated him according to the Law. The priests alone had the authority to declare someone cured of leprosy after checks had been carried out, but Jesus' authority went further than that. According to Mark, he could actually perform the healing. Most important of all, this touch would have given back to the man a sense of being human and being cared about, and restored his dignity.

This incident is full of emotion. The man's desperate state aroused Jesus' compassion. Jesus wanted the man to go without delay for the certificate of cure that would ensure his acceptance by society. He also did not want attention being drawn to his powers, although Mark later tells us that the man was so happy he could not help telling people about his cure.

Objectives

Investigate why those suffering from leprosy were, and often still are, excluded from society.

Study the story of Jesus healing a man with leprosy and consider what this shows about Jesus' mission.

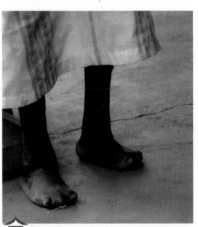

A *Leprosy can be a disfiguring disease*

Activity

Read Leviticus 13:45–46. What were the rules for someone with leprosy? What effect do you think these rules would have had on those who had the disease?

Father Damien

In the 19th century Fr Damien, a Belgian priest who was working in Hawaii, asked to be sent to the island of Molokai. This was a colony for those with leprosy. When he arrived, he was appalled at their miserable existence, just waiting for death. He organised the building of huts for them to live in, a church for worship, and for regular supplies of food to be dropped off at the shore. He transformed the lives of all who were there. One day in his sermon, he said, 'We, who have leprosy …' and the colony realised that now he, too, had the disease. When he heard, Fr Damien's bishop wanted him to leave the island, as a treatment had been developed for those whose leprosy was in its early stages. But Fr Damien refused. He continued to serve his fellow sufferers until he died. Throughout his life on Molokai, Fr Damien's aim was to reflect the love and compassion of Jesus.

B   *Father Damien*

C   *Fr Damien helped those with leprosy on the island of Molokai*

D   *The Leprosy Mission logo reminds us that Jesus, filled with compassion, reached out and touched the man with leprosy*

Research activity 🔍

The Leprosy Mission

Find out about the work in the 21st century of the Leprosy Mission by going onto one of its websites, noted in the Links below. How do its workers reflect Jesus' compassion in what they say and do?

∞ links

Information about the work of the Leprosy Mission can be found at:
www.leprosymission.org. or www.leprosymission.org.uk

Summary

You should now understand attitudes to leprosy in the time of Jesus, and know Mark's account of the healing of the man suffering from leprosy. You should understand what this shows about the Person of Jesus and his mission.

Study tip

Understanding why Jesus touched the man who had leprosy will also help you with questions relating to the Person of Jesus. Christians believe that he was fully human as well as fully divine, and this story highlights his human emotions.

5.8 Jesus and the outcast (3)

Introduction

In practice, most Jews at the time of Jesus could not avoid some dealings with Gentiles. Strict Jews, however, kept any contact to an absolute minimum, to avoid becoming unclean.

The Greek woman's daughter (Mark 7:24–30)

Beliefs and teachings

Jesus left that place and went to the vicinity of Tyre. He entered a house and did not want anyone to know it; yet he could not keep his presence secret. In fact, as soon as she heard about him, a woman whose little daughter was possessed by an evil spirit came and fell at his feet. The woman was a Greek, born in Syrian Phoenicia. She begged Jesus to drive the demon out of her daughter. 'First let the children eat all they want,' he told her, 'for it is not right to take the children's bread and toss it to their dogs.' 'Yes, Lord,' she replied, 'but even the dogs under the table eat the children's crumbs.' Then he told her, 'For such a reply, you may go; the demon has left your daughter.' She went home and found her child lying on the bed, and the demon gone.

Mark 7:24–30

Jesus' decision to leave Galilee and go into mainly Gentile territory might have been to avoid the authorities. It was not to conduct a mission to the Gentiles: Jesus' mission was primarily to the Jews, to bring them back to God so that they could take the gospel further afield. Jesus did not want news of his presence to spread, for fear that people would regard him as just another of the many wandering healers, some of whom were 'con men'. This explains his apparent rudeness to the woman when she came, asking him to cure her daughter. Using a Jewish proverb that referred to Jews as the children and Gentiles as dogs, Jesus stated that the Jews must have access to his teaching first. The woman accepted what he said. Her reply made the point that the Jews were already being offered the good news, and so Gentiles like her could now be offered it too. It showed her conviction that Jesus' authority was God-given and Jesus was impressed. Her faith was rewarded, and its depth was shown in her trust that her daughter was cured, without her having seen this happen.

The significance of Jesus' attitude to outcasts

For Christians in the 1st century

Mark introduced his writing as the good news about Jesus. His gospel gave hope and encouragement to 1st-century Christians facing the possibility of persecution. Equally importantly, it assured them that they were all valued by God. Those who were slaves were despised in the secular world, and even more so if they were Christian. Many 1st-century Christians faced discrimination on a daily basis.

A *Illustration on a stamp of the ruins of ancient Tyre, where Jesus healed the Greek woman's daughter*

For Christians in the 21st century

The world in the 21st century also has divided communities. Different groups suffer injustice for a wide variety of reasons, such as race, religion, appearance, social status, or gender. Jesus' attitude to those who were despised shows that for Christians **prejudice** and **discrimination** are unacceptable. Jesus accepted people as they were. He made a point of seeking out and befriending those who were excluded from society, giving them a sense of their dignity and worth as human beings. Christians believe that Jesus' attitude should be reflected within the Christian community today. Some devote their lives to the cause of **justice**, pressuring communities, employers and governments to recognise the right of all humans to fair and equal treatment.

B   *Christians believe that all human beings are of equal worth*

Research activity

Sybil Phoenix

Sybil Phoenix is a Christian who has helped many young people who felt excluded by society. Research her life and work on the internet and create a personal profile of her. Include information on her background, how she knows what it is like to be treated as an outcast by society, what groups she has helped and how. To conclude your profile, include your view of how she reflects the example of Jesus in her life.

All human beings are important

> 66 *There is only one race that really matters, the human race to which we all belong.* 99
>
> *Sybil Phoenix interview*

Study tip

Many set texts in Mark's Gospel show Jesus responding to those who were outcast. Ensure you know and understand these texts. This will enable you to answer in more detail if you are asked about Jesus' attitude to outcasts.

Summary

You should now know and understand the story of Jesus' meeting with the Greek woman. You should also understand the impact of Jesus' attitude to outcast groups on Christian beliefs and practice today.

5.9 Jesus and the sick (1)

◼ Introduction

Although Jesus discouraged people from telling others about his healings, they were nevertheless an important part of his ministry. They showed not only his power but his compassion, and demonstrated the good news of the coming Kingdom of God. Faith played an important part in the healings, although it was not always referred to directly. Sometimes it was the faith of the person being healed that was commented on; at other times it was the faith of friends or relatives. On one occasion, the limited faith shown by a father was sufficient for Jesus to heal his epileptic son.

When Jesus returned to his home town of Nazareth from the area around the Sea of Galilee where many of his healings took place, he was rejected by most people. They had known him all his life and could not believe that he was anyone special. This meant he could not perform many miracles. Mark commented that Jesus was taken aback by the lack of faith. The impression given by Mark's Gospel is that faith was rewarded with healing, but that it was not an absolute condition of healing.

∞ links

Read what was written about Jesus the miracle worker on pages 76–77, 96–97, 106–109 and 112–115.

Read what was written about Jesus the miracle worker on pages 76–77, 96–97, 106–109 and 112–115.

Objectives

Explore the significance of faith in the healing stories recorded in Mark's Gospel.

Study Jesus' healing of the woman with a haemorrhage.

Activity

1 This task is intended to reinforce your knowledge of set texts that contain healings by Jesus. It will also help you see the extent to which faith was important in each of them. (You will study more of these stories in detail later in this chapter.)

 a Create a table with four columns. Give the columns the following headings: 'Reference', 'Healing', 'Status of faith' and 'Jesus' comment on faith'. In the first column, under the heading 'Reference', list the following set texts in Mark: 1:40–44; 2:1–12; 3:1–6; 5:21–24, 35–43; 5:25–34; 7:24–30; 10:46–52.

 b Complete the table: in the second column simply name the healing; in the third column indicate whose faith (if any) was clearly present; and in the final column quote anything Jesus said about faith in each of the stories. (If there is nothing to write, simply put a dash.)

Extension activity

Create a table identical to the one you made for the activity above, but this time using the following texts: 1:29–31; 7:31–37; 8:22–26; 9:14–29. These are not set texts, but studying them will deepen your knowledge and understanding of the role of faith in Jesus' healings. Read also Mark 6:1–6 and write in your own words why the citizens of Nazareth rejected Jesus' claim to have God-given authority and how that affected him and his ministry there.

A *Many Christians believe that faith is important for healing*

■ The woman with a haemorrhage (Mark 5: 25–34)

Beliefs and teachings

And a woman was there who had been subject to bleeding for twelve years. She had suffered a great deal under the care of many doctors and had spent all she had, yet instead of getting better she grew worse. When she heard about Jesus, she came up behind him in the crowd and touched his cloak, because she thought, 'If I just touch his clothes, I will be healed.' Immediately her bleeding stopped and she felt in her body that she was freed from her suffering. At once Jesus realised that power had gone out from him. He turned around in the crowd and asked, 'Who touched my clothes?' 'You see the people crowding against you,' his disciples answered, 'and yet you can ask, "Who touched me?"' But Jesus kept looking around to see who had done it. Then the woman, knowing what had happened to her, came and fell at his feet and, trembling with fear, told him the whole truth. He said to her, 'Daughter, your faith has healed you. Go in peace and be freed from your suffering.'

Mark 5:25–34

The woman's condition (vaginal bleeding) made her unclean, according to the Jewish laws, and an outcast from society. She should not have approached Jesus in the crowd that had gathered about him as he was on his way to heal Jairus' daughter. Nor should she have touched him, for this would make him unclean. That is why she was so secretive. Touching his garment was not superstitious; in the ancient world, clothing was seen as an extension of someone's personality. So, in effect, she was touching Jesus himself.

Jesus realised someone had drawn on his powers by touching him. The disciples' impatience contrasted with Jesus' determination to know who had sought his help. The woman's fear was probably a mixture of awe at the realisation that she was cured and concern that Jesus might be angry at her touching him without permission, as she was a woman and had been ritually unclean. His final words to her made it clear that her faith had led to her cure. She was healed by his touch, before he spoke to her. That healing was more than physical. The word 'peace' referred to wholeness of life. She was healed in body and soul.

B *Christians believe that faith may lead to a cure at Lourdes*

Activity

2 Read Mark 5:25–34. Then, from memory, describe the healing of the woman with a haemorrhage. When you have finished, check your account for accuracy.

Summary

You should now know Mark's story of the woman with a haemorrhage and understand the part that faith played in Jesus' healings. You should be able to use a variety of texts to demonstrate that role of faith.

Study tip

If you are asked to explain the importance of faith in the healing miracles, do not state that faith was essential to healing. It is more accurate to say that on many occasions it was important for healing.

5.10 Jesus and the sick (2)

Jairus' daughter (Mark 5:21–24, 35–43)

Beliefs and teachings

When Jesus had again crossed over by boat to the other side of the lake, a large crowd gathered around him while he was by the lake. Then one of the synagogue rulers, named Jairus, came there. Seeing Jesus, he fell at his feet and pleaded earnestly with him, 'My little daughter is dying. Please come and put your hands on her so that she will be healed and live.' So Jesus went with him. A large crowd followed and pressed around him … .

While Jesus was still speaking, some men came from the house of Jairus, the synagogue ruler. 'Your daughter is dead,' they said. 'Why bother the teacher any more?' Ignoring what they said, Jesus told the synagogue ruler, 'Don't be afraid; just believe.' He did not let anyone follow him except Peter, James and John the brother of James. When they came to the home of the synagogue ruler, Jesus saw a commotion, with people crying and wailing loudly. He went in and said to them, 'Why all this commotion and wailing? The child is not dead but asleep.' But they laughed at him. After he put them all out, he took the child's father and mother and the disciples who were with him, and went in where the child was. He took her by the hand and said to her, 'Talitha koum!' (which means, 'Little girl, I say to you, get up!'). Immediately the girl stood up and walked around (she was twelve years old). At this they were completely astonished. He gave strict orders not to let anyone know about this, and told them to give her something to eat.

Mark 5:21–24, 35–43

Objectives

Study Mark's story of Jairus' daughter.

Explore different views on what happened and the importance for Christians of this incident.

B *Jairus came to Jesus while he was by the shores of Lake Galilee*

A *Jesus healing Jairus' daughter*

In his community, Jairus was a religious leader, so it is surprising that he sought Jesus' help. His absolute desperation was revealed when he fell at Jesus' feet. It was while Jesus was on the way to Jairus' home that the incident of the woman with a haemorrhage took place. The faith shown by Jairus after he received news of the girl's death contrasted with the mockery of the mourners. Wanting privacy, Jesus allowed only the girl's parents and his three closest disciples into where the girl lay. The details suggest that Mark got his information from Peter. Jesus' gentleness was vividly remembered: Jesus took the girl by the hand, the Aramaic word *talitha* means literally 'little lamb' and he told her parents to give her food. Presumably the command to secrecy related to the details of the cure.

Activity

1 **a** Work in groups of three. One of you is Jairus; one is his wife; and the third is another synagogue official who is not sympathetic to Jesus. The official comes to Jairus' house a few days after the miracle and questions Jairus and his wife. The official cannot understand how Jairus could have sought the help of such a man as Jesus.

   Work out between you what the official might say; how Jairus might justify his actions; what the views of his wife who has also witnessed the incident might be; and how the discussion might continue.

b Perform your role play for the rest of the class.

c Discuss the different views represented as a class.

■ The significance of this story for Christians

Some Christians find it hard to believe that Jesus raised the girl from the dead. Scientifically, it is not possible. Some, therefore, think that she was in a state of deep unconsciousness. They think that Jesus' words to the professional mourners who had already arrived at the house suggest he thought this was the case.

Some think that the incident never actually happened, but that it was a kind of parable, showing that death is not the end.

There are many Christians, however, who would claim that as Jesus was the Son of God, anything was possible for him. If Jesus could himself rise from the dead, then he could raise someone else from the dead. They believe that the incident happened just as Mark described it.

Whichever of these views is correct, the story is important for Christians, showing the greatness of the power of God and giving hope that there is life after death. Many Christians believe that Jesus' statement that the girl was sleeping was very appropriate since death is not the end but leads to eternal life with God. They believe that after death they will be reunited with God.

Discussion activity

1 Discuss the following questions in pairs or small groups.

   a Do you think it matters for Christians whether or not the incident happened as Mark told it?

   b Do you think that the meaning is more important to Christians than the detail?

Summary

You should now know the story relating to Jairus' daughter and differing Christian views on what happened. You should also appreciate its importance for many Christians today.

∞links

To help you understand the people in the activity, read pages 32–33.

C *Christians believe that they will be reunited with God after death*

Study tip

It is important not just to know the story of Jairus' daughter in detail, but also to understand what it means for many Christians.

5.11 Jesus and the sick (3)

■ The healing of blind Bartimaeus (Mark 10:46–52)

Beliefs and teachings

Then they came to Jericho. As Jesus and his disciples, together with a large crowd, were leaving the city, a blind man, Bartimaeus (that is, the Son of Timaeus), was sitting by the roadside begging. When he heard that it was Jesus of Nazareth, he began to shout. 'Jesus, Son of David, have mercy on me!' Many rebuked him and told him to be quiet, but he shouted all the more, 'Son of David, have mercy on me!' Jesus stopped and said, 'Call him.' So they called to the blind man, 'Cheer up! On your feet! He's calling you.' Throwing his cloak aside, he jumped to his feet and came to Jesus. 'What do you want me to do for you?' Jesus asked him. The blind man said, 'Rabbi, I want to see.' 'Go,' said Jesus, 'your faith has healed you.' Immediately he received his sight and followed Jesus along the road.

Mark 10:46–52

Objectives

Study Mark's account of the healing of Bartimaeus.

Explore the debate between believers in miracles and those who think that science makes it difficult to believe in them.

On the surface, this is another story of Jesus healing someone who turned to him for help. But this story, like so many, has deeper significance throughout. When Bartimaeus shouted 'Son of David', this might have made the crowd nervous; he was declaring his faith in Jesus as the Messiah, and such a public declaration of Jesus' identity was dangerous. Many present tried to silence him. They might also have been impatient, thinking that Jesus was too important to bother with a beggar. In contrast, Jesus stopped, and made time for someone who needed him. Bartimaeus' faith was shown in the way he abandoned his cloak (which he would have used for collecting his begging money) to go to Jesus. Jesus' question seems odd, but presumably he wanted the blind man to have a part in his own cure. Bartimaeus is told that his faith has saved him, signifying both physical and spiritual healing.

The reference to Bartimaeus following Jesus along the road has a double meaning. When he was blind, Bartimaeus would not have been allowed into the men's part of the Temple. He now literally accompanied Jesus to Jerusalem, able at last to enter the Court of Israel. 'The Way' was also the earliest name for the Christian faith and Mark might have also meant that Bartimaeus followed Jesus as a disciple.

A *Jericho, where Bartimaeus was healed*

Activities

1. In what ways was Bartimaeus almost like an outcast in Jewish society?
2. Why was it dangerous to shout 'Son of David'?
3. How could Jesus tell that Bartimaeus had faith?
4. Explain the two meanings of 'Your faith has saved you.'
5. Which of these two meanings do you think is the more important? Give reasons for your opinion.

∞ links

See pages 50–51 for the entry into Jerusalem.

Extension activity

Mark's placing of the story about the healing of the blind man just before the conversation near Caesarea Philippi pointed to the importance of that event as showing two levels of belief in Jesus: that of the general public and that of Peter. In the same way, just before Jesus entered Jerusalem, Mark recorded the healing of another blind man, Bartimaeus. His calling to Jesus as 'Son of David' (i.e. Messiah) points to the significance of Jesus' entry into that city as Messiah.

a   Read about the entry to Jerusalem (see the Links on page 114) and look for similarities between Mark's telling of those events and the story of the healing of Bartimaeus given above. Look particularly at Mark 10:47 and 11:10.

■ Miracles and science

For those who believe that Mark's Gospel was directly inspired by God, there is no problem with believing in Jesus' miracles: Jesus was the Son of God, and so had the power to perform them, using his authority to challenge the laws of nature.

For many Christians, however, it is difficult to believe that Jesus did perform miracles. They contradict the laws of science, which themselves were put in place by God. Experience shows that a crowd cannot be fed with a tiny amount of food, that a blind person's sight cannot be restored just by words, and that a dead girl cannot be raised to life. Some Christians, therefore, think that some of these stories were created by the Church as symbols of religious truth. They think that 'truth' covers more than just literal, historical or scientific truth. Stories that were created to show that God has the power to transform lives and give hope, or to teach that death is not the end, are religious truths.

Others think that Jesus did have healing powers, in the same way that some people today, known as faith healers, are believed to have that gift. They also point out that the power of the mind to overcome physical limitations is enormous. Faith (on the part of the healer and/or the person being healed) and a positive attitude **can** make all the difference.

Research activities 🔍

Lourdes

1   Divide into three groups. Using the Lourdes website listed in the Links, or a search engine, each group should research an aspect of Lourdes, a place where Christians believe that healing can occur, finding out about:

■ Bernadette and how and why Lourdes became a place of pilgrimage for sick people.

■ What happens on a pilgrimage there today?

■ The procedure for declaring that a miraculous cure has taken place and also about the case of Anna Sanataniello.

2   Each group should then give a brief presentation to the rest of the class on what they have discovered.

Summary

You should now know and understand the story of blind Bartimaeus and the significance of miracles, and be starting to consider whether miracles are possible or whether modern science makes belief in them impossible.

Discussion activity 👥👥👥

In small groups, read again some of the healing miracles recorded in Mark's Gospel, and the paragraph above on 'Miracles and science'. What do you think? Could miracles have happened? Give reasons for your views.

⬭⬭ links

To help you with the discussion activity, read about Jesus' healing miracles on pages 77, 96–97 and pages 106–107.

⬭⬭ links

The Lourdes website is at: www.lourdes-france.org.

B   *Sick and disabled pilgrims at Lourdes today*

Study tip

Make sure that you think about whether or not Jesus could have performed miracles and be sure that you can refer to some examples. You might be asked for your views on this in an exam.

5

Jesus' relationships with others – summary

For the examination, you should now be able to:

✔ understand why Jesus came into conflict with the religious authorities over Sabbath laws, the use of the Temple Court and the payment of tax to Caesar, with particular reference to the following stories:
  – the man with the paralysed hand (Mark 3:1–6)
  – the incident in the Temple Court (Mark 11:15–18)
  – payment of taxes to Caesar (Mark 12:13–17)

✔ understand the significance of this conflict and these stories for modern Christian attitudes to religious and secular authority and the issue of violent and non-violent protest

✔ understand Jesus' attitude to outcast groups, with particular reference to the following stories:
  – the man with leprosy (Mark 1:40–44)
  – the call of Levi and eating with sinners (Mark 2:13–17)
  – the Greek woman's daughter (Mark 7:24–30)

✔ understand the significance of Jesus' attitude in these stories for modern Christian attitudes to justice, equality, prejudice and discrimination

✔ understand Jesus' attitude to those who were sick, with particular reference to the following stories:
  – Jairus' daughter (Mark 5:21–24, 35–43)
  – the woman with a haemorrhage (Mark 5:25–34)
  – blind Bartimaeus (Mark 10: 46–52)

✔ understand the relationship between faith and healing and the debate concerning miracles and science.

Sample answer

1 Write an answer to the following exam question:

Describe in detail the healing of blind Bartimaeus. *(6 marks)*

2 a Read the sample answer below:

> Bartimaeus was begging in Jericho when he heard that Jesus was passing by. He shouted, 'Son of David, have mercy on me' and kept on shouting, even when the people around tried to silence him. Jesus stopped when he heard and told the crowd to call him. When Bartimaeus was told Jesus wanted him, he leapt up. Casting his cloak to one side, he made his way to Jesus. When Jesus

> asked what he wanted, he asked for his sight. Jesus said, 'Your faith has cured you', and Bartimaeus could see. He then followed Jesus along the road to Jerusalem.

b With a partner, discuss the sample answer. This is a detailed account. Do you think the student has written enough to gain a good mark? Do you think that there are other things that the student could have included in the answer?

c What mark would give this answer out of 6? Look at the mark scheme in the Introduction on page 7 (AO1). What are the reasons for the mark you have given?

Practice questions

TAX COLLECTORS ARE DISHONEST AND DO NOT KEEP THE LAW. IF WE MIX WITH THEM, WE'LL BECOME LIKE THEM.

OUR ORAL TRADITIONS TELL US THAT WE SHOULD NOT HEAL ON THE SABBATH UNLESS LIFE IS IN DANGER.

IF YOU TRUST SOMEONE, YOU TRUST THEIR POWER TO HELP YOU. A POSITIVE ATTITUDE CAN MAKE A HUGE DIFFERENCE.

1   Name the tax-collector whom Jesus called to be a disciple.   *(1 mark)*

2   How did Jesus defend himself when criticised for eating with tax collectors and sinners?   *(2 marks)*

3   Explain why Jesus and the religious authorities disagreed about the Sabbath law.   *(6 marks)*

> **Study tip**   Questions asking you to 'explain' might carry a number of marks. You need to answer in detail. Remember to develop every point you make. You should make relevant reference to Mark's Gospel.

4   'People cannot be healed if they do not have faith.' Do you agree? Give reasons for your answer, showing that you have thought about more than one point of view. Refer to Christianity in your answer.   *(6 marks)*

> **Study tip**   Do not forget to include religious comment in a 6-mark evaluation answer. For example, you could quote Jesus' comment on faith in one of the set texts you have studied. Otherwise you will not reach more than Level 3.

6 Discipleship

6.1 The Twelve: the calling of the first four disciples

The Twelve

The word disciple is used for anyone in any century who is a follower of Jesus. So in his lifetime Jesus had countless disciples. But it was common for 1st-century rabbis to have around them a small group of men to whom they gave special teaching. At an early point in his ministry Jesus chose twelve men, often referred to simply as **the Twelve**. According to Mark, he chose them to be with him (presumably as companions and to share his experiences); to be sent out to preach; and to have the authority to drive out demons. Three of the Twelve (Peter, James and John) became especially close to him and they alone experienced some of the most significant moments in Jesus' ministry.

∞ links

For the moments of significance Peter, James and John alone shared with Jesus, read pages 46–47 and 56–57.

The call of the disciples (Mark 1:16–20)

The first four disciples were fishermen. The Sea of Galilee had a very good supply of fish and the villages bordering the lake specialised in curing fish to be sold throughout Palestine and beyond. Fishermen were not the kind of men you might have expected to be chosen to take the good news throughout Israel and ultimately to the world. Presumably Jesus already knew them and realised their potential.

Simon Peter (known as Peter) and Andrew, the first two to be called, worked with a casting net. This circular net had stones fastened around its edge to weigh it down and a draw rope to pull it closed. James and John were probably part of a bigger operation, as their father had hired men to help him. James and John were certainly not poor; Peter and Andrew probably also made a reasonable income.

A 'Come, follow me, and I will make you fishers of men.'

Discussion activity

If you were suddenly asked to stop everything to join someone in a venture, would you do it? What might you want to know first? If you had been among these four fishermen, what might your response to Jesus' call have been? Peter was married and probably the others were also. They would still have spent time at home when in Capernaum, but they had to give up secure jobs and leave their families for many days at a time to follow Jesus. Do you think they were right to do that?

The significance of the call

Mark was making two important points in his account of their call. Firstly, these four men were not just to become followers of Jesus; they were to share in his ministry, as for instance when Jesus sent the disciples out in pairs on a preaching and healing mission. Ultimately, they were not just 'fishers of men' in Galilee; at the commission they were authorised as leaders to take the gospel to the world. (This was unusual: disciples usually simply learned the rabbis' teaching and passed it on.) Secondly, they recognised Jesus' authority and their response to his call was immediate. Here Mark was highlighting both the authority that Jesus possessed and the obedience of the four men.

Modern discipleship

Discipleship is important for all Christians.

Study tip

As you learn about the Twelve, note what the stories reveal about their response to Jesus and the demands he made of them. You might be asked to explain what these stories can teach Christians about the nature of discipleship.

Key terms

Discipleship: following Jesus in his lifetime; to be an active believer in Jesus.

∞ links

Read about the commission on pages 70–71 and 122–123.

Read about the commission on pages 70–71 and 122–123.

Case study

Bishop Hugh Montefiore

Hugh Montefiore was born in 1920 into a famous Jewish family. He went to Rugby School, where one evening in his study, when he was 16, he saw a figure in white coming towards him and saying, 'Follow me.' He believed this was Jesus, though he knew little about Christianity. His response was immediate, and from that moment on he was a Christian as well as a Jew.

He studied theology, became a priest, and for many years worked in the university system. He was eventually made a bishop, first of Kingston-upon-Thames and then of Birmingham. He was concerned for the underdog, supported the ordination of women and was involved in sorting out racial and industrial problems in Birmingham. He was also very concerned about the environment and about nuclear weapons. He retired long before he needed to, to care for his wife, who was suffering from Alzheimer's disease. From that evening in his study in 1936 until his death in 2005 he was a faithful and devoted disciple of Christ.

B *Bishop Hugh Montefiore*

Activity

Find out more about Hugh Montefiore by reading some of the obituaries posted on the internet. In what ways was his personality similar to that of Peter? If you find this hard to answer, remind yourself of Peter's nature by reading pages 42–47.

If you find this hard to answer, remind yourself of Peter's nature by reading pages 42–47.

Summary

You should now know about Jesus' call of the first four disciples and about a similar modern example of a call to Christian discipleship.

The Twelve: the mission

The mission of the Twelve (Mark 6:7–13)

Beliefs and teachings

Calling the Twelve to him, he sent them out two by two and gave them authority over evil spirits. These were his instructions: 'Take nothing for the journey except a staff – no bread, no bag, no money in your belts. Wear sandals but not an extra tunic. Whenever you enter a house, stay there until you leave that town. And if any place will not welcome you or listen to you, shake the dust off your feet when you leave, as a testimony against them.' They went out and preached that people should repent. They drove out many demons and anointed many sick people with oil and healed them.

Mark 6:7–13

Objectives

Study the mission of the Twelve.

Examine its implications for Christian disciples today.

Significance of the mission

Jesus sent out the Twelve to help him with his mission of preaching and healing. According to Mark's Gospel, Jesus spent much of his time travelling around Galilee, preaching the good news about the Kingdom of God. As part of this mission, he also healed people and cast out demons. Perhaps Jesus knew that time for him was short, and he wanted the disciples to help him reach as many people as possible in the time left.

Only the bare essentials

He allowed them to take only what was essential: a staff, a kind of walking stick to help them over rough terrain; and sandals, so that cut feet would not slow them down. Jesus wanted his disciples to rely on God, trusting, as Jesus himself did, that he would provide for their needs. This was an important lesson to learn for the future, when they would no longer have Jesus' physical presence to support them.

Acceptance and rejection

They were to stay wherever hospitality was first offered and not move on to better accommodation. Jesus was making it clear that they were not on a holiday. If rejected, they were to leave peaceably, but publicly to shake off the dust from their feet as they left. Jews returning from a trip abroad did this as they re-entered Israel, to prevent foreign dust from contaminating Jewish soil. So the disciples' action showed that those who rejected them were excluded from the new chosen people and should change their minds before it was too late. Jesus had sent them off in pairs: to support one another, but also because any account of an event, under Jewish law, needed two witnesses.

The three aspects to their mission

The first aspect of the mission was the disciples' message of repentance, which reflected Jesus' own message. Exorcism – 'authority over evil spirits' – was an important part of Jesus' own ministry, and the disciples were given the authority to share in this. Anointing sick people with oil was often used for healing in the 1st century, and the disciples were given authority to do this as well. These three aspects were to be a central part of Jesus' commission after his resurrection.

A *The disciples were allowed sandals for their journey*

∞links

Read about Jesus' commission later in this chapter on pages 122–123 and also on pages 70–71.

Mission in the 21st century

There are many Christian organisations committed to proclaiming God's love. This is sometimes by preaching, but often by helping those in need, whether in this country or in less developed countries. Sometimes workers are given accommodation and sufficient money for essentials. Others might be volunteers who even have to fund themselves. Those involved in Christian mission are encouraged to rely, like the Twelve, on God's goodness.

Discussion activity

The Twelve came from very different backgrounds and had different personalities. Matthew was a tax collector who had worked for the Romans. Simon the Zealot (not Simon Peter) was a nationalist, committed to the overthrow of Roman rule in Judaea.

a   Work in pairs. Imagine that these two were paired together for the mission. What would it have been like for them, being together for 24 hours a day? How do you think they would have learned to get on with each other? What might each have contributed to the success of their mission?

Extension activity

Find out more about the work of volunteers on Mercy Ships UK by going onto their website. Read again what is written on this page about mission in the 21st century, and think about what this means for those volunteers. How is their work a continuation of the mission of Jesus and of the Twelve? In what ways will they, like the disciples, need to trust that God will help them? Create a poster advertising for volunteers. You will need to include what they do and also the fact that they will have to fund themselves, and why.

∞ links

To find out about Mercy Ships UK, go to: **www.mercyships.org.uk**.

B *Mercy Ships UK provides free surgeries*

Mercy Ships UK

Case study

Mercy Ships UK is a Christian charity committed to helping the most needy people in the world. On its website it states that it seeks to 'reflect the love of Jesus' and to 'become the face of love in action, bringing hope and healing to the poor'. In 1982 the first Mercy Ship set sail. Its name was *Anastasis*, a Greek word meaning 'resurrection'. It was a hospital ship equipped with three operating theatres and a 40-bed ward. On board were 350 volunteers: doctors, nurses, cooks, etc. All of them had to pay for everything they needed during their time on the ship, including food.

There are now several ships, going to over 150 places giving medical treatment. There are also land-based programmes aimed at rehabilitating communities torn apart by war; improving water supplies and sanitation; and training people in disease prevention.

Study tip

When you are learning Mark's story of the mission of the Twelve, make sure that you do not confuse it with his account of their commission. This mistake is very common in exams.

Summary

You should now know the story of the mission of the Twelve and know how Christians today seek to follow their example.

Peter's promise (Mark 14:26–31)

Beliefs and teachings

When they had sung a hymn, they went out to the Mount of Olives. 'You will all fall away,' Jesus told them, 'for it is written: "I will strike the shepherd, and the sheep will be scattered." But after I have risen, I will go ahead of you into Galilee.' Peter declared, 'Even if all fall away, I will not.' 'I tell you the truth,' Jesus answered, 'today – yes, tonight – before the cock crows twice you yourself will disown me three times.' But Peter insisted emphatically, 'Even if I have to die with you, I will never disown you.' And all the others said the same.

Mark 14:26–31

At the end of the Last Supper, Jesus and his disciples went to Gethsemane. Jesus' use of an Old Testament quotation referring to the shepherd being struck and his sheep scattered made it clear that his death was part of God's plan and that he accepted it. At the same time it implied that all would be well: Jesus would gather his disciples to him again just as the shepherd would gather his flock. Peter's impulsive personality and his genuine devotion to Jesus come across vividly in his reaction. Peter, himself, remembered very clearly what he had said after he later denied Jesus.

Peter's denials (Mark 14:66–72)

Beliefs and teachings

While Peter was below in the courtyard, one of the servant girls of the high priest came by. When she saw Peter warming himself, she looked closely at him. 'You also were with that Nazarene, Jesus,' she said. But he denied it. 'I don't know or understand what you're talking about,' he said, and went out into the entrance. When the servant girl saw him there, she said again to those standing around, 'This fellow is one of them.' Again he denied it. After a little while, those standing near said to Peter, 'Surely you are one of them, for you are a Galilean.' He began to call down curses on himself, and he swore to them, 'I don't know this man you're talking about.' Immediately the cock crowed the second time. Then Peter remembered the word Jesus had spoken to him: 'Before the cock crows twice you will disown me three times.' And he broke down and wept.

Mark 14:66–72

His denial of Jesus must have been carved into Peter's memory for the rest of his life. The girl's recognition of him posed absolutely no threat. A woman's evidence was not valid, and she was just a servant. Peter had thought better of running away in Gethsemane. He had gone to the high priest's palace to see what would happen to Jesus. But now, terrified that he would be arrested like Jesus, Peter denied all knowledge of him. When someone commented on his Galilean dialect, he reacted even more strongly. When the cock crowed for the second time, however, he broke down, as he remembered Jesus' words earlier that evening and his response to them.

Objectives

Explore what led to Peter's denials of Jesus, despite his promise to die with him if necessary.

Consider Peter as a role model for Christians.

∞ links

Read how 'the sheep were scattered' at Jesus' arrest on pages 56–57.

A *The church built at the site of Peter's denials*

B   *Two views of Peter: a weathercock, placed on church towers as a reminder of Peter's denials; and St Peter's Square/Basilica in Rome, commemorating him*

Activity

Read again Mark 14: 26–31, 66–72 and the information on this page. Then, from memory, write a detailed account of Peter's promise and denials. When you have finished, check your work for accuracy.

Extension activity

1   **a**   Create a bullet-point fact file on Peter. Use the following Bible references from Mark's Gospel: 1:16–18, 30–31; 5:37–43; 8:27–33; 9:2–8; 10:23–31; 14:27–31, 32–39, 50, 54, 66–72; 16:6–8 to gather information. You might have studied some of these passages already. All except 1:30–31 are set texts.

   b   What might Peter have learned from the experiences described in these texts that might have helped him when he became leader of the Christian community?

Discussion activity

Work in pairs. Some people think Peter's threefold denial that he had ever known Jesus was just as bad as Judas' betrayal. They think that he is, therefore, a poor role model for Christians to follow. What do you think? In deciding this, it might help to think about both the positive and negative things you have learned about Peter.

Summary

You should now know the stories of Peter's promise and denials. You should be starting to evaluate Peter's fitness to be a leader of the Christian community and a role model for Christians.

∞ links

Read more about role models on pages 124–125.

Study tip

In an exam you might be required to evaluate the example Peter set for later Christians. You need to be prepared for such a question.

The Twelve: role models

■ The commission (Mark 16:14–18)

The commission marks a new start for the 11 disciples who were left after Jesus' crucifixion and resurrection. They had misunderstood Jesus during his ministry, and failed him in the lead up to his trials and crucifixion. But Jesus understood that they were human, with human weaknesses, and he knew they had the potential to become leaders of the Christian Church. So in this meeting the risen Jesus gave them their orders: to preach the gospel to everyone.

What happened next?

The history of the early Christian community and the 1st-century Church shows that the disciples did not let Jesus down. They became respected leaders, fearlessly proclaiming their belief that Jesus was the Son of God. It is commonly accepted that most of them died as martyrs. Peter became the first pope (bishop of Rome) and died in the Neronian persecutions of the 1st century. Many Christians think that the faith that Jesus showed in them at the commission, despite their earlier failings, was justified.

■ The Twelve in Mark's Gospel

In stories featuring the Twelve, Mark certainly pointed out their failings. There were, however, occasions when they worked well. Many Christians feel that they can relate to the disciples because they were not perfect, and that the way the disciples overcame their failings makes them good **role models** for people today.

■ 21st-century role models

In today's world, celebrities are very influential. Young people, in particular, look up to their favourite pop stars, sports stars, actors and models. They might be strongly influenced by their attitudes and opinions. Christian young people are no exception. They also are influenced by famous people, both Christian and non-Christian. Some celebrities recognise that they have an opportunity to change the world for the better and use their fame for this purpose. They are aware of the responsibility that comes with fame.

Objectives

Explore the importance of the Twelve as role models.

Consider the influence of celebrities as role models on young people today.

∞ links

Read Mark 16:14–18 and an explanation of the commission on pages 70–71.

Key terms

Role model: people who others follow and try to copy in their actions or beliefs.

∞ links

Read about the Neronian persecutions on pages 22–23.

A *Peter is a role model for Christians all over the world*

The high points	
The four fishermen and Levi responded immediately to Jesus' call	Mark 1:16–20; 2:14
They gave up everything to follow him	Mark 10:28
The twelve went on a mission exorcising demons and healing sick people	Mark 6:12–13
Peter wanted to honour Jesus at the transfiguration	Mark 9:5
Peter regretted running away when Jesus was arrested, and went to find out what would happen to him	Mark 14:54
They were sure they would be loyal even if it meant death.	Mark 14:31
They were upset that Jesus' said one of them would betray him	Mark 14: 18–19
Peter recognised Jesus as the Messiah	Mark 8:29

The low points

They lacked faith during the storm on Lake Galilee	Mark 4:35–41
They argued with Jesus before he fed the five thousand	Mark 6:37
Peter did not accept what Jesus said about the Son of Man having to suffer	Mark 8:32–33
Peter, James and John kept falling asleep in Gethsemane	Mark 14:37–41
They did not believe Jesus was alive after the Resurrection	Mark 16:10–11, 13
Three times Peter denied knowing Jesus	Mark 14:66–71
They all ran away when Jesus was arrested	Mark 14:50
Judas betrayed Jesus	Mark 14:10–11, 43–44

Discussion activity

Discuss in pairs whether you think that Jesus was right to give the 11 disciples the chance to carry out his commission, after they had let him down. Give reasons for your opinion.

Study tip

If asked to assess whether Peter is a good role model for Christians, make clear reference to incidents from Mark's Gospel, such as those noted above. Ensure that you have thought about these and developed your opinion before the exam.

Case study

Diane Louise Jordan

Diane Louise Jordan is an actress who for many years was a Blue Peter presenter. Diane is a Christian and has presented many *Songs of Praise* programmes. She is the vice president of the Action for Children trust and is involved with many charities, such as the Oasis Trust and Children in Need. Most recently she has become known for her friendship with a Scottish man released from Death Row in the US. On his return to the UK, he was in need of support and Diane befriended him, helping him to reintegrate into society.

Research activity

The Constant Gardener Trust

Find out how the stars and directors of the film *The Constant Gardener*, set in Kenya, decided to help the people where the film was made. The website gives information about their projects.

∞ links

Use this website to help with the research activity:
www.constantgardenertrust.org.

Extension activities

1. In small groups research the following celebrities: Bono, Elijah Wood, Angelina Jolie and Lenny Henry.
2. Explain why Christians might be influenced by them. Do you think Christians should only be influenced by Christian celebrities, or by anyone working to make the world a better place?

B *Celebrities like Angelina Jolie can use their fame for good*

Summary

You should now understand how Mark's Gospel presents both the strengths and weaknesses of the Twelve. You should also understand their significance as role models for Christians, and the influence of modern celebrities as role models.

The Kingdom of God

The Kingdom of God was central to Jesus' teaching and is a key theme in Mark's Gospel. The term did not refer to a place where God reigned but to his rule over people. The Old Testament claimed that God ruled over the earth. But not everyone accepted him as their king **yet**. God's reign was, therefore, both a present reality and a future hope. Jesus taught that the Kingdom was both already here, and was also still to come, in the sense that everyone was obeying God. The term was also linked to Jesus' ministry. In his life and death Jesus was fully obedient to God. This showed that God's rule was here and now; it was a present reality. God's Kingdom was also extended to outcasts and Gentiles. At the same time, those who rejected Jesus' God-given authority risked future judgement.

Why did Jesus use parables?

Jesus often taught about the Kingdom of God in **parables**. The stories were drawn from everyday life. This made his teaching easier to understand and remember, and encouraged people to apply his teaching to their own lives. Jesus' parables contained both the assurance that God was in control, and the challenge to respond.

The parable of the Sower (Mark 4:3–9, 14–20)

∞ links

Read the set passages in Mark 4:3–9, 14–20 before continuing with this section.

This parable gave reassurance that despite many setbacks, the Kingdom of God would triumph. Jesus' followers need not worry about the negative response of so many people to him and his teaching.

B *The meaning in the details of the parable of the Sower*

Detail	Meaning
The farmer scatters the seed.	The seed is the word of God.
The seed on the path is eaten by birds.	The listener does not respond, or is tempted away by Satan so it is wasted.
The seed on rocky ground cannot grow deep roots. It grows but is scorched by the sun and dies.	The listener's enthusiasm is killed off by persecution and other troubles.
The seed on thorny ground is choked by the weeds.	The listener's response is stifled by materialism and worldly concerns.
The seed on fertile ground produces a bumper harvest.	The listener has a positive response, in belief and action.

A *Seed sown on fertile soil results in a bumper harvest*

Activity

1. Read again Mark 4:3–9, 14–20 and Table B. Then, from memory, retell the parable of the Sower and the explanation that Jesus gave of it. Check your account for accuracy.

Discussion activity 👥

1. Working in pairs, apply the meaning behind the parable of the Sower to life in 21st-century Britain. What kind of people would be those from whom 'Satan comes and takes away the word'? What would be a modern equivalent of the persecution Jesus refers to?

The parable of the Mustard Seed (Mark 4:30–32)

∞links

Read the set text in Mark 4:30–32 before continuing with this section.

Mustard seeds are very small. Jesus was teaching that despite the limited response to his mission, God was in control and his rule would become worldwide. Birds were sometimes used as a Jewish symbol for Gentiles, so this parable shows the Kingdom offering protection to Gentiles as well as Jews. First-century Christians in Rome must have found this very reassuring. The good news started with a Galilean rabbi and 12 humble followers. The Christian community was still small and being persecuted. Yet, one day, God's rule would be acknowledged by everyone.

C *Tiny mustard seeds grow into a large shrub*

The growth of the Kingdom of God in the modern world

After the Communist revolutions in China and what became known as the Soviet Union, Christians in those countries were persecuted for much of the 20th century. Officially, both nations were atheist; all religions were regarded as superstition and many places of worship were closed. Many Christians found themselves in labour camps or in prison. They were tortured and some were even killed. When Communism gave way to democracy in the Soviet Union, people were free to practise their religion openly and it became clear that the persecution had not destroyed Christianity. In China, licensed religions are now permitted, and Christians are a small but committed group.

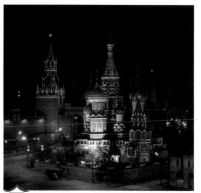

D *Persecution did not destroy Christianity: St Basil's Cathedral, in the heart of Moscow's Red Square, and a church in China*

Activity

2 Divide into small groups. Make up a modern version of the parable of the Sower that relates to 21st-century life. Turn it into a play to be performed for the rest of the class.

Study tip

Answers on the parable of the Sower often confuse the meaning of the seed on rocky ground with that on the path or choked by thorns. Learn the details on the chart so that your answer is accurate.

Summary

You should now understand the term 'Kingdom of God' and know the parables of the Sower and the Mustard Seed, and their meanings. You should also be starting to evaluate the relevance of Jesus' parables to 21st-century Christians.

The Kingdom of God: the cost of discipleship

◼ The cost of discipleship (Mark 8:34–38)

Beliefs and teachings

Then he called the crowd to him along with his disciples and said: 'If anyone would come after me, he must deny himself and take up his cross and follow me. For whoever wants to save his life will lose it, but whoever loses his life for me and for the gospel will save it. What good is it for a man to gain the whole world, yet forfeit his soul? Or what can a man give in exchange for his soul? If anyone is ashamed of me and my words in this adulterous and sinful generation, the Son of Man will be ashamed of him when he comes in his Father's glory with the holy angels.

Mark 8:34–38

A *'If anyone would come after me, he must … take up his cross'*

According to Mark, this teaching came immediately after Jesus' insistence that Messiahship involved rejection, suffering and death. Jesus now used dramatic metaphorical language to show his audience that following him was not easy. It involved being willing to make sacrifices; self-interest had no place in discipleship. (Those who were listening would almost certainly have had in mind the image of a condemned criminal carrying the crossbeam of the cross on the way to execution. At this point, his disciples did not know that this was literally to be Jesus' fate.) It was a shocking image to use but Jesus wanted to warn his followers of the shame and disgrace they might have to experience. Followers of Jesus would have to tread the same path as he did, i.e. the path of suffering that he had outlined to the Twelve shortly before. Those who put **materialist** comfort and pleasure first ran the risk of losing what really mattered: eternal life in God's Kingdom. Rejection of Jesus would lead to judgement when Jesus returned as the glorious Son of Man at the Second Coming.

Objectives

Study Jesus' teaching on the cost of discipleship.

Consider its significance for 1st- and 21st-century Christians.

∞ links

Read more about Jesus' crucifixion on pages 62–67; the title 'Son of Man', pages 86–89; Jesus' teaching on materialism, pages 130–131.

Key terms

Materialist: used to describe someone who has a great interest in possessions, money and wealth.

Activities

1. What three things did Christians have to be willing to do, according to Jesus' teaching?

2. Why was the image of taking up the cross so shocking?

3. 'If anyone would come after me he must … follow me' seems to state the obvious. What did Jesus mean?

Cost of discipleship for 1st-century Christians

Almost all the Twelve became martyrs, and died for their beliefs. By the time Mark wrote his gospel, James had been beheaded and Peter crucified. Mark's readers knew that they, too, might face persecution and death at any time. They faced ridicule and hostility on a daily basis. Mark sought to encourage them in his gospel by pointing out that Jesus had foreseen all this; it was all part of being a disciple. They should never forget, though, that for Jesus death was not the end. Those who remained faithful to him would share in the joys of the Kingdom of God, whether in this life or the life to come.

'Alexamenos worships his god'

Case study

In archaeological excavations, a graffito was found on the wall of an ancient Roman building showing a crucified figure with a donkey's head. See if you can find this image by using the internet. At one time the building was part of the emperor's palace and some have suggested it was the servants' quarters. It may go back to the 1st century, so it is possible that Alexamenos was a Christian slave living at the time Mark wrote his gospel. It is thought that a fellow slave scratched this drawing onto the wall, with the writing quoted above. The crucified figure with a donkey's head made it clear what the 'artist' thought about the Christian faith and those who followed it.

Cost of discipleship for 21st-century Christians

For many Christians, Jesus' teaching on the cost of discipleship is hard to apply in today's world. Some, however, take Jesus' words about self-denial very seriously, devoting their entire lives to God by becoming monks or nuns. They live in communities, sometimes cut off from the rest of society, devoting their lives to prayer and study as well as working to supply their daily needs. They make vows, promising to own no personal possessions, never to marry and to obey the leader of their monastery. For them, the Kingdom of God is a reality. For most Christians, however, it is simply a matter of trying to be faithful to God in their daily lives and thinking about others' needs as well as their own.

⊂⊃ links

Read more about the possible cost of discipleship for today's Christians on pages 26–27.

Research activity

St Hugh's Charterhouse

Find out about the monks living in this monastery by going onto their website, given in the Links opposite. In what ways could it be said that they deny themselves and take up their cross? Why do they live such a solitary life?

⊂⊃ links

The website for St Hugh's Charterhouse is at: www.parkminster.org.uk.

Summary

You should now know Jesus' teaching on the cost of discipleship and understand its significance for 1st- and 21st-century Christians.

Study tip

Remember that Jesus was using a metaphor in his teaching on the cost of discipleship. He did not mean it to be taken literally. Think about how his teaching might apply to the lives of ordinary Christians today.

The Kingdom of God: the rich man and wealth

The rich man (Mark:10:17–22)

Beliefs and teachings

As Jesus started on his way, a man ran up to him and fell on his knees before him. 'Good teacher,' he asked, what must I do to inherit eternal life?' 'Why do you call me good?' Jesus answered. 'No-one is good – except God alone. You know the commandments: "Do not murder, do not commit adultery, do not steal, do not give false testimony, do not defraud, honour your father and mother."' 'Teacher,' he declared, 'all these I have kept since I was a boy.' Jesus looked at him and loved him. 'One thing you lack,' he said. 'Go, sell everything you have and give to the poor, and you will have treasure in heaven. Then come, follow me.' At this the man's face fell. He went away sad, because he had great wealth.

Mark 10:17–22

Jesus might have suspected at first that the man's words were mere flattery, and so he just told him to keep the commandments. But then Jesus could see the man's sincerity. He could also see what the problem was: the man was too attached to his possessions.

Discussion activity

1   On other occasions, Jesus did not tell people they had to sell all they had to the poor in order to become disciples. Why do you think he did so on this occasion? Work in pairs to discuss this.

Jesus' teaching on wealth (Mark 10:23–27)

Beliefs and teachings

Jesus looked around and said to his disciples, 'How hard it is for the rich to enter the kingdom of God!' The disciples were amazed at his words. But Jesus said again, 'Children, how hard it is to enter the kingdom of God! It is easier for a camel to go through the eye of a needle than for a rich man to enter the kingdom of God.' The disciples were even more amazed, and said to each other, 'Who then can be saved?' Jesus looked at them and said, 'With man this is impossible, but not with God; all things are possible with God.'

Mark 10:23–27

The disciples' amazement at Jesus' teaching on wealth sprang from the Jewish belief that wealth was a sign of God's approval. Jesus, however, believed that wealth could get in the way of a person's relationship with God. He used a very vivid image to get his point across (though some scholars suggest he was thinking of a very narrow gate into Jerusalem rather than an actual needle). For Jesus, the possibility of entering the Kingdom was more thanks to God's goodness and love than something human beings could earn.

Objectives

Study the conversation between Jesus and the rich man.

Know and understand Jesus' teaching about wealth and on making sacrifices for the Kingdom of God.

Explore possible benefits and problems that might arise for those who are wealthy.

A   *For some people, money is everything*

B   *Imagine getting this through the eye of a needle!*

Rewards in the Kingdom of God (Mark 10:28–31)

Beliefs and teachings

Peter said to him, 'We have left everything to follow you!' 'I tell you the truth,' Jesus replied, 'no-one who has left home or brothers or sisters or mother or father or children or fields for me and the gospel will fail to receive a hundred times as much in this present age (homes, brothers, sisters, mothers, children and fields – and with them, persecutions) and in the age to come, eternal life. But many who are first will be last, and the last first.'

Mark 10:28–31

Jesus reassured his disciples that sacrifices would be more than compensated for in the Kingdom of God, both in the present and in the future, though persecutions would be part of life. Status in the Kingdom of God would be vastly different from how it was on earth.

Activity

1 a Make a list of the benefits of money and possessions. Next to it make a list of the problems they can cause.

   b Compare your list with that of the person sitting nearest you. Do you think the benefits outweigh the problems?

Research activity

Rich philanthropists

A philanthropist is someone who cares about other human beings, and who often gives large sums of money away to help others. Use the internet to research Bill and Melinda Gates. Find out why they are giving so much away and to whom.

Extension activity

Use the internet to find out about Sir Tom Hunter, a Scottish businessman and philanthropist. What projects is the Hunter Foundation committed to? Sir Tom said that he would leave some money to his three teenage children, but that he would not 'burden them with wealth'? What do you think he meant by this? How do you think you would feel about this if you were one of his children?

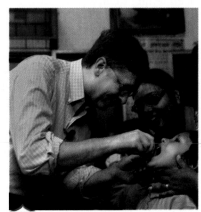

C *Bill Gates administers an oral polio vaccine to a child*

Discussion activity

2 In small groups discuss Jesus' teaching about the problems of wealth. Modern Western society is very materialist. Do you think Jesus' teaching has any relevance in today's world? Is it practical for someone to give up everything to go to where the need is greatest?

Summary

You should now understand the story of the rich man and Jesus' teaching on wealth and rewards for those who make sacrifices. You should also be able to assess the relevance of his teaching to life in modern society.

Study tip

When evaluating the importance of money, remember to take into account that money is needed for the essentials of life, e.g. food, clothing and shelter. So beware of simply saying that having money is wrong.

Jesus' teaching on service (Mark 10:42–45)

Beliefs and teachings

Jesus called them together and said, 'You know that those who are regarded as rulers of the Gentiles lord it over them, and their high officials exercise authority over them. Not so with you. Instead, whoever wants to become great among you must be your servant, and whoever wants to be first must be slave of all. For even the Son of Man did not come to be served, but to serve, and to give his life as a ransom for many.'

Mark 10:42–45

Objectives

Study Jesus' teaching on service.

Examine its significance for 21st-century Christians.

Jesus gave this teaching on **service** because there had been an argument between the disciples. James and John had come to Jesus, asking for the seats of honour at the Messianic Banquet, the feast that would celebrate the recognition of Jesus as Messiah. The others were furious, not perhaps because they saw anything wrong in what the two brothers had asked for, but because they had got their request in first. This shows how little the Twelve really understood Jesus, for he had been telling them that following the Messiah involved suffering.

So now Jesus tried to make it crystal clear. The values of the Kingdom of God were the opposite of those in the secular world. In the Roman Empire, greatness was all about power, domination and status. In the Kingdom of God it was about self-giving service. Those who wanted to be truly great must follow the example of Jesus. His whole life had been based on serving others, and soon, in some mysterious way, his death would save humanity (in Aramaic, the 'many' in the Bible reference meant 'all'). Jesus had in mind here the Suffering Servant referred to in Isaiah. That Suffering Servant would be hated and despised by others and he would undergo a humiliating death. Yet, eventually, people would recognise that his suffering and death had been for them, and he would be honoured.

Key terms

Service: self-giving help to others.

A *In the Roman Empire, being great meant being powerful*

Activity

1   a   Read through Chapters 4 and 5 in this book, and make a list of the different occasions when Jesus served others during his ministry.

    b   In what ways did he serve people?

The significance of Jesus' teaching for Christians

Sometimes the Christian Church, like all human institutions, has been concerned with power and status. Yet Jesus' teaching is clear: Christians are meant to be more concerned with humble, self-giving service. Jesus taught that it is in everyday deeds of kindness that the Kingdom of God is clearly seen. On an earlier occasion he had told his disciples that the simple act of giving someone a cup of water would have an eternal reward. Throughout the centuries, there have been Christians who have taken Jesus' teaching seriously, by helping others in their communities.

∞links

Read about Isaiah's Suffering Servant in Isaiah 53:2–5.

∞links

Jesus' teaching about an eternal reward for a simple act of kindness is found in Mark 9:41.

Research activity

The Society of St Vincent de Paul (SVP)

The SVP is a Roman Catholic organisation committed to serving others in communities at home. Find out what its members do by going onto its website and clicking on 'Visiting and Befriending'. Many Roman Catholic schools have youth SVP groups. Find out about the kinds of things they do by going onto the Youth SVP website and clicking on 'our works'.

links

Links for the SVP are: www.svp.org.uk and www.youthsvp.org.uk.

B   *A Youth SVP summer camp*

Case study

Mother Maria of Ravensbruck (1891–1945)

Maria was born in Latvia and her original name was Elizabeth. Her family moved to Russia, where her father died, and for a time she became an atheist. Her first marriage ended in divorce and eventually she remarried. By this time, her Christian faith had returned. She and her family had to leave Russia during the Communist revolution because their lives were in danger. Like many other Russian refugees they went to Paris, where she had a son, Yuri. She became a nun, taking the name Mother Maria, but did not live in a convent. Instead, her home was a centre for the poor, providing a soup kitchen, a shelter and a chapel. She was helped by Yuri and a Russian Orthodox priest. They began to help Jews to escape when the Nazis took over Paris. In 1942 Jewish children were rounded up in the Velodrome d'Hiver. Mother Maria rescued some of the children in rubbish bins. Although she knew that she was being watched by the Gestapo, she continued to help Jews. In 1943 she, Yuri and the priest were arrested. She was sent to Ravensbruck concentration camp, where she continued to help her fellow prisoners, giving whatever food she had to others. On Good Friday in 1945, she took the place of a Jewish prisoner and went to her death in the gas chamber.

links

Examples of self-giving service: James Mawdsley, page 27; Oscar Romero, page 27, Fr Damien, page 107; Sybil Phoenix, page 109; Mercy Ships UK, page 121; Mother Teresa, page 135; Sister Helen Prejean page 137.

> *There is one moment when you start burning with love and you have the inner desire to throw yourself at the feet of some other human being. This one moment is enough. Immediately you know that instead of losing your life, it is being given back to you twofold.*
>
> *Mother Maria of Ravensbruck*

Study tip

You are required to know about a modern example of self-sacrifice and service. You could use Mother Maria, or one of the others included in this book (see Links above).

Summary

You should now know Jesus' teaching on service and understand how some modern Christians have applied that teaching to their lives.

The Kingdom of God: the greatest commandments

The greatest commandments (Mark 12:28–34)

Objectives

Study Jesus' teaching on the greatest commandments.

Explore its significance for Christians.

Beliefs and teachings

One of the teachers of the law came and heard them debating. Noticing that Jesus had given them a good answer, he asked him, 'Of all the commandments, which is the most important?' 'The most important one,' answered Jesus, 'is this: "Hear, O Israel, the Lord our God, the Lord is one. Love the Lord your God with all your heart and with all your soul and with all your mind and with all your strength." The second is this: "Love your neighbour as yourself." There is no commandment greater than these.' 'Well said, teacher,' the man replied. 'You are right in saying that God is one and there is no other but him. To love him with all your heart, with all your understanding and with all your strength, and to love your neighbour as yourself is more important than all burnt offerings and sacrifices.' When Jesus saw that he had answered wisely, he said to him, 'You are not far from the kingdom of God.' And from then on no-one dared ask him any more questions.

Mark 12:28–34

'Which is the most important commandment?' was a genuine question. There were said to be 365 prohibitions and 248 positive commands in the Torah, and rabbis were constantly looking for one principle that would cover all these rules. Jesus first quoted from the *Shema*, which all Jews should say daily. The *Shema* states that there is only one God, who must be loved with total commitment. His second statement was a quotation from the Old Testament book Leviticus. For Jesus, no commandments were greater than those and they went together. By 'neighbour' Jesus would have meant all those living in Israel, both Jew and Gentile. The scribe's statement was surprising, as the sacrificial system was central to Jewish religion. Jesus praised his attitude. He made it clear that a person's first duty was to love God with total commitment, and from this love would come a love for his fellow people.

∞ links

You will find the *Shema* in Deuteronomy 6:4–9.

Beliefs and teachings

Do not seek revenge or bear a grudge against anyone among your people, but love your neighbour as yourself. I am the LORD.

Leviticus 19:18

A *The words from the Shema, quoted by Jesus*

B *The scroll in a mezuzah contains the Shema*

Activity

Read Mark 12:28–34 and what is written about it on these pages. Then give an account of Jesus' conversation with the scribe. Check what you have written for accuracy.

The importance of Jesus' teaching for Christians

Many times in the New Testament, love of God and your neighbour are presented as, together, being essential for any follower of Jesus. Christians have tried to follow these commands throughout the centuries.

Case study

Mother Teresa (1910–97)

Mother Teresa (originally called Agnes) came from Albania. She joined a convent in Ireland, from where she was sent to teach in a convent school in Calcutta (Kolkata), India. She was very happy there, but one day on a train, she felt God calling her to serve 'the poorest of the poor'. Once she was given permission, she moved out of the convent and formed the Missionaries of Charity. They lead a very simple life that is centred round love of God and love of neighbour. Each day they say Mass and then go out to rescue abandoned babies, tend the sick, care for the dying, etc. Missionaries of Charity can be found all over the world, wherever there is desperate need. In 1979, Mother Teresa was awarded the Nobel Peace Prize, which she accepted in the name of the poor. She asked for the celebration dinner to be cancelled and for the money it would have cost to be given, along with her prize money, to those in need.

C *This postage stamp from India, where Mother Teresa worked, celebrates her being awarded the Nobel Peace Prize*

Extension activity

Find out more about Mother Teresa by researching on the internet. A useful site is listed in the Links below. Create a magazine article about her, entitled: 'The woman who loved God and neighbour'. Do not just give the story of her life. Make sure that your article shows the ways in which she followed Jesus' teaching about love of God and neighbour.

∞ links

For information on the life and work of Mother Teresa go to: www.request. org.uk. Click on the main site, then on 'History', and find 'Mother Teresa' in the '20th and 21st Centuries' section.

The need for love

> 66 *In these twenty years of work ... I have come more and more to realize that it is being unwanted that is the worst disease that any human being can ever experience ... For all kinds of diseases there are medicines and cures. But for being unwanted, except there are willing hands to serve and there's a loving heart to love, I don't think this terrible disease can ever be cured.* 99
>
> *Mother Teresa,* Something Beautiful for God

D *Mother Teresa worked for the very poor in India*

Study tip

Make sure that you know this important conversation. You may be asked to retell it, and explain its meaning. It is also an important passage to include in questions about the nature of the Kingdom of God.

Summary

You should now know Jesus' teaching on the greatest commandments, and understand its meaning and importance for Christians.

The Kingdom of God: the widow at the treasury

The widow at the treasury (Mark 12:41–44)

Beliefs and teachings

Jesus sat down opposite the place where the offerings were put and watched the crowd putting their money into the temple treasury. Many rich people threw in large amounts. But a poor widow came and put in two very small copper coins, worth only a fraction of a penny. Calling his disciples to him, Jesus said, 'I tell you the truth, this poor widow has put more into the treasury than all the others. They all gave out of their wealth; but she, out of her poverty, put in everything – all she had to live on.'

Mark 12:41–44

Objectives

Study Mark's story of the widow at the treasury.

Explore the significance of Jesus' teaching for Christians.

Around the Court of the Women there were 13 offering boxes for the upkeep of the Temple. They were known as the 'Trumpets' because of their shape. Jesus and his disciples saw a number of wealthy people making huge offerings. In contrast, the coins the widow gave were leptons, the smallest in circulation in Palestine, less than a sixtieth of a labourer's daily pay. But to such a poor woman they would have had great value.

Just as Jesus praised the woman who anointed him with expensive oil as a sign of her devotion, so he now praised this poor widow for the sacrifice she made. It was a sign of her commitment to God and her complete trust that he would provide for her. For some, his praise would have made little sense. She was a woman and a widow, and such people were often overlooked in 1st-century society.

A *The widow offered two leptons, almost worthless coins*

Discussion activity 👤👤👤

Have a whole-class discussion about Jesus' teaching. He said that the woman had given everything she had. He could not have known whether she had other coins at home, so he could not have meant this literally. What do you think he meant?

Jesus also would not have known the personal circumstances of the rich people or the proportion of their total wealth that they gave. What do you think was the difference between their offerings and hers?

The meaning of Jesus' teaching

Jesus' teaching was all about motivation. He knew that the two coins the widow gave would not have paid for a single nail needed to maintain the Temple. He was not interested in the size of the offerings. What mattered to him was that the offering was given out of pure love for God, as an act of self-giving, not of looking for praise.

Its significance for Christians today

Many Christians believe that in their daily lives they should show the same commitment and devotion. For some Christians, this might mean giving everything up to live a life of dedication to God and humanity, like Mother Teresa. Most Christians think in terms of giving up time to deepen their spiritual lives by prayer or Bible study. They might devote time to visiting a lonely person or writing to someone in prison who has no family to care about him or her. The **form** of the giving is not important; it is the **motivation** behind it.

Activity

1. a   Work in groups of eight. Imagine that you are taking part in a chat show. One of you is the presenter. Three are the following guests: the rich man, the woman who anointed Jesus, and the widow. The others make up the audience, who will be invited to join in. The presenter should discuss with each guest what happened in the story relating to them and how they feel about Jesus' response to them. The discussion should then be opened up to the audience for questions and comment. For instance, was Jesus unfair to the rich man, and did he expect too much? Should the woman have sold the ointment and given the money to charity? Would that have been a better use of it? Was Jesus' praise for the widow's offering 'over the top', since what she gave was worthless?

   b   At the end of the chat show, the presenter should note the different views that have been expressed and report back to the rest of the class.

∞ links

For this activity, read Mark 10:17–22; 14:3–9; pages 52–53 and page 128–129 in this book; and the beliefs and teachings box on page 136.

Study tip

It is important to understand ways in which Christians today show commitment and devotion to God. Use the example of Sister Helen Prejean as a starting point for thinking of other ways.

Research activity 🔍

Sister Helen Prejean CSJ

1. a   Sister Helen is an American nun who was working among the 'throwaways' (her word) of society when she was asked to write to someone on Death Row. Find out about her life and her views from the internet or from watching the film *Dead Man Walking*. Her commitment is not shown through giving away all her money. In what ways is it shown?

   b   What do you think Christians might learn from her commitment?

B   *Sister Helen Prejean has devoted her life to those facing the death penalty*

Commitment to service

> ❝ *People ask me all the time, 'What are you, a nun, doing getting involved with these murderers?' You know how people have these stereotypical ideas about nuns: nuns teach; nuns nurse the sick.*
>
> *I tell people to go back to the gospel. Look at who Jesus hung out with: lepers, prostitutes, thieves – the throwaways of his day. If we call ourselves Jesus' disciples, we too have to keep ministering to the marginated, the throwaways, the lepers of today. And there are no more marginated, thrown-away, and leprous people in our society than death-row inmates.* ❞
>
> Sister Helen Prejean

Summary

You should now know the story about the widow at the treasury and understand its importance for Christians. You should also be able to suggest how Christians might apply this teaching to their everyday lives.

6

Discipleship – summary

For the examination, you should now be able to:

✓ give an account of the following stories relating to the Twelve:
- the call of the disciples (Mark 1:16–20)
- the mission of the Twelve (Mark 6:7–13)
- Peter's promise and denials (Mark 14:26–31, 66–72)
- the commission (Mark 16:14–18)

✓ understand the significance of these stories for 21st-century Christians, and the function of modern leaders and celebrities as role models

✓ explain the meaning of the term 'Kingdom of God' and Jesus' teaching on the Kingdom, with particular reference to the following passages:
- parables of the Kingdom (Mark 4:3–9, 14–20, 30–32)
- the costs of discipleship (Mark 8:34–38)
- the rich man and wealth (Mark 10:17–31)
- Jesus' teaching on service (Mark 10:42–45)
- Jesus' teaching on the greatest commandments (Mark 12:28–34)
- the widow at the treasury (Mark 12:41–44)

✓ understand the significance for 21st-century Christians of Jesus' teaching on the nature of the Kingdom and discipleship.

Sample answer

1 Write an answer to the following exam question:

'It is wrong for Christians to be rich.' Do you agree? Give reasons for your answer, showing that you have thought about more than one point of view. (6 marks)

2 Read the following sample answer:

> I agree. Christians should not be rich as they tend to think more about money than about God. They also cannot cope with life if something happens and they are no longer rich. Sometimes marriages break up because the husband or wife is made redundant and they feel that

> they can no longer enjoy the lifestyle they had.
>
> I disagree. Some Christians do not forget about God when they are rich. They still pray and go to church regularly. They also give generously to charity.

3 With a partner, discuss the sample answer. To achieve the top level you need to give a 'well-argued response'. How do you think this answer could be improved, so that it is better argued?

4 What mark would you give this answer out of 6? Look at the mark scheme in the Introduction on page 7 (AO2). What are the reasons for the mark you have given?

Practice questions

1 Jesus gave the answer shown in the illustration above when asked a question by a scribe. What was the question? *(1 mark)*

2 Explain how Christians today might be faithful disciples of Jesus in their everyday lives. *(6 marks)*

3 Give an account of the parable of the Mustard Seed. *(3 marks)*

4 What does this parable teach about the Kingdom of God? *(3 marks)*

> **Study tip** Make sure that you read questions carefully and give a focused and relevant answer. Note how many marks are available. You should not write three lines when 6 marks are available, or half a page for a 2-mark question.

Glossary

Anointing: the Old Testament custom of pouring oil onto kings' heads at their coronation came to have Messianic significance. Mark saw the anointing of Jesus at Bethany as a sign that he was the Messiah.

Ascension: the event after the resurrection, when Jesus returned to God, the Father, in heaven.

Authority: Christians believe that the gospels should be respected as conveying deep religious truths.

Baptism: the sacrament through which people become members of the Church; in Mark's Gospel, John the Baptist used baptism as a way of washing away sins in readiness for the coming of the Messiah. He also baptised Jesus, though this was not connected with washing away of sin.

Bible: sacred book for Christians containing both the Old and New Testaments.

Centurion: an important officer in the Roman Army. A centurion was present at Jesus' crucifixion.

Christ: the leader promised by God to the Jews. The word literally means 'Anointed One' in Greek; the Hebrew equivalent is Messiah. Christians believe Jesus to be the Christ.

Christian: someone who believes in Jesus Christ and follows the religion based on his teachings.

Commandment: a rule for living, given by God; one of the Ten Commandments; Jesus said that the greatest commandments were love of God and of neighbour.

Commission: the occasion, after the Resurrection, when the risen Jesus told the Eleven to preach the good news to the whole world.

Cross: a Christian symbol, based on the sacrifice of Jesus at his crucifixion; the object on which Jesus was crucified.

Crucifixion: Roman method of execution by which criminals were fixed to a cross; the execution and death of Jesus on Good Friday.

Disciples: followers of Jesus; this term is often used to refer the first twelve followers of Jesus; any Christian, in any age, who lives their life according to Gospel values.

Discipleship: following Jesus during his lifetime; to be an active believer in Jesus.

Discrimination: to treat someone or something differently either favouring or denying something, e.g. not allowing lepers to be part of the community in Mark's Gospel.

Elijah: an Old Testament prophet. It was believed that he would come to help good people in trouble and return to prepare the way for the Messiah.

Equality: treating every person in a way that ensures justice and fairness.

Faith: belief and trust in someone, e.g. Jesus.

Gethsemane: garden outside Jerusalem where Jesus prayed before his arrest and execution.

Golgotha: literally 'Skull Hill'; it is the place where Jesus was crucified.

Gospel: literally 'good news', there are four Gospels telling of the life and work of Jesus.

Haemorrhage: severe loss of blood.

Herodians: these people were supporters of the Herod family.

Holy Spirit: the third person of the Holy Trinity who descended like a dove on Jesus at his baptism. Christians believe that the Holy Spirit is present and inspires them.

Jesus: 1st century Jewish teacher and holy man, believed by Christians to be the Son of God.

Justice: ensuring that all are treated fairly and their rights are upheld.

Kingdom of God: wherever God is honoured as king and his authority accepted; Jesus taught about the Kingdom of God both on earth and in heaven. The rule of God.

Last Supper: the final meal that Jesus ate with his disciples, on the evening before his execution. It was based on the Jewish Passover and is the basis of Holy Communion today.

Leprosy: a disease of the skin. Those who had leprosy were treated as outcasts.

Materialist: used to describe someone who has a great interest in possessions, money and wealth.

Messiah: the person whom God will send to save humanity, believed by Christians to be Jesus (the Anointed One). Hebrew form of the word 'Christ'.

Ministry: this word means 'service'. When used with reference to Jesus, it refers to his three years' work of teaching and healing. His ministry began with his baptism and ended with his crucifixion.

Miracle: an event that lies beyond normal human knowledge and understanding. It is an unexplained event with religious significance.

Moses: the man who rescued the Jews from Egypt and received the Ten Commandments from God.

N

Non-violent protest: a demonstration or other action which draws attention to wrong without resorting to violence.

O

Outcasts: those who were rejected by others in society, e.g. lepers, and not given fair treatment.

P

Parables: stories told by Jesus that have spiritual meanings.

The Passion: the term used to describe Jesus' suffering prior to his death.

Passion predictions: Jesus' reference on a number of occasions to his immanent suffering and death. He often ended these predictions with a reference to his future glory.

Persecution: to be treated badly, e.g. arrested, tortured, killed, denied rights as a result of one's beliefs.

Person of Jesus: the identity of Jesus, e.g. Christians believe he was the Messiah.

Peter: the leading Apostle. Peter was the 'rock' on which Jesus based the Church and was the first Pope.

Pharisees: devout Jewish religious leaders whose lives centred around the keeping of the Jewish law. They came into conflict with Jesus many times on matters relating to the law.

Prejudice: to be in favour or against someone or something without evidence. To pre-judge.

R

The Resurrection: when Jesus rose from the dead after dying on the cross. One of the key beliefs of Christianity.

Role models: people who others follow and try to copy in their actions or beliefs.

S

Sabbath: the Jewish day of rest, from sunset on Friday to sunset on Saturday.

Satan: the evil force that tempts people, also known as the Devil.

Scribes: known as 'doctors of the Law', they were the experts in the Jewish Law at the time of Jesus.

Secular: a set of beliefs which does not need to have God or religion in them.

Service: self-giving help to others.

Son of David: a title used about Jesus. Christians believe that Jesus fulfilled the Old Testament prophecy that the Messiah would be a descendant of King David.

Son of God: a title used for Jesus; Christians believe that before his birth as a human being, Jesus had always existed as God the Son. Also as used by the centurion after Jesus' death; means 'a Righteous Man'.

Son of Man: a title used by Jesus of himself. In the Old Testament, the title was used of a heavenly being from God. Jesus used the title to stress that he was more than simply a human being and that he came with authority from God. Jesus also linked the title with suffering and service.

Source: a text, statement, person, etc. that supplied information.

Synagogue: where Jews meet for worship on the Sabbath. Jesus regularly attended the synagogue.

T

The Temple: the most sacred Jewish place of worship. It was in Jerusalem. The Romans destroyed it in 70CE. Mark states that when Jesus died, the Temple curtain was torn in two.

Transfiguration: an incident in the New Testament when Jesus was lit up by divine light, through which the divinity of Jesus was revealed (Mark 9:2–9).

The treasury: the part of the Temple where the Temple Tax was paid by worshippers.

The Twelve: the twelve men chosen by Jesus to help with his ministry.

V

Violent protest: demonstration or other action which draws attention to a wrong using violence.

W

'Watershed' events: something which happens that changes the course of history or someone's life.

Index

A

Alexamenos 129
Andrew 118
angels 40
anointing at Bethany 52–53
Antipas 30, 43
Ascension 71, **140**
atonement 67
authority 8, 102–103

B

baptism of Jesus 38–39, 91
Barabbas 61
Barnabas 17
Bartimaeus 15, 114
Bethany, anointing at 52–53
betrayal of Jesus 53, 54, 57
bible 140
blind man at Bethsaida, healing of 44
Bonheoffer, Dietrich 103

C

Caesarea Philippi 42–45, 84
Carey, William 39
Cassidy, Sheila 45
centurion at Jesus' crucifixion 65, **140**
Christ 82–85
  Christians
  1st century 22–23, 24–25, 101, 108, 129
  21st century 26–27, 109, 129
  and authority 102–103
  early Church 12, 13, 20–21
  and Jesus' baptism 39
  and Jesus in Gethsemane 57
  and Jesus' temptation 41
  and Last Supper 55
  and love 135
  and meaning of Jesus' death 66–67
  and mission 121
  motivation 137
  and protest 99
  and the Resurrection 72
  and service 132–133
  and story of Jairus' daughter 113
  and titles for Jesus 85, 89, 91
  and the transfiguration 47
Church of England 102
commandments 94, 134–135, **140**

commission 70–71, 124
converts 20
crucifixion 19, 25, **62–65**

D

Damien, Father 107
Daniel, Book of 87
David, King 51, 82
disciples 14
  and the commission 70–71
  failings of 19, 25, 70
  and Jesus as Messiah 42, 44
  and Last Supper 55
  and the Resurrection 68, 70
  see also **Twelve, the**
discipleship 19, **119**
  cost of 128–129, 131
discrimination 109
doves 38

E

Elijah 46, 65, **140**
equality 140
Eucharist 22, 81
exorcisms 77
Ezekiel 86

F

faith 110, **140**
five thousand, feeding 78–81

G

Gentiles 12, 98, 108
Gethsemane 56–57, **140**
Golgotha 62, **140**
gospel 8
Greek woman's daughter 108

H

haemorrhage, woman with 111
healings 44, 77, 110–115
heresy 20
Herod 30
Herodians 33, 96, 100, **140**
Holy Communion 55, 81
Holy Spirit, 140

J

Jairus, daughter of 14, 112

James 46, 47, 56, 57, 118
Jerusalem, entry into 50–51
Jesus
  anointing at Bethany 52–53
  baptism 38–39, 91
  crucifixion and burial 19, 62–67
  entry into Jerusalem 50–51
  feeding the five thousand 78–81
  in Gethsemane 56–57
  identity of 18
  and Jewish authorities 33, 96–97, 98–99, 100
  on Kingdom of God 126–127, 130–131, 132, 134
  Last Supper 54–55
  Messiah 42, 44, 51, 82–85
  miracle worker 77, 79
  and outcasts 104–105, 106, 108
  overview of ministry 36–37
  Resurrection 19, 68–73
  and the sick 110–115
  Son of God 38, 46, 59, 90–91
  Son of Man 42, 44, 54, 86–89
  teacher 76, 78–79, 126–127
  temptation of 40–41
  transfiguration 46–47
  trials 59, 60–61
  and the Twelve 118–119, 120, 122
Jewish Council *see* Sanhedrin
John 46, 47, 56, 57, 67, 118
John the Baptist 30, 38
Jordan, Diane Louise 125
Joseph of Arimathea 67
Judas 53, 57
justice 109

K

Kingdom of God 20, 126
  cost of discipleship 128–129
  greatest commandments 134–135
  Messianic Banquet 55
  and motivation 136–137
  parables and 126–127
  and service 132–133
  and wealth 130–131

L

Last Supper 54–55, **140**
Lent 41
leprosy 106–107, **140**
Levi, the call of 104
love 66, 135

M

manna 80
Maria of Ravenbruck, Mother 133
Mark 10, 11, 69
Mary Magdalene 68, 70
materialist 128
Matthew's Gospel 16
Mawdsley, James 27
Mercy Ships UK 121
Messiah 12, 42, 44, 51, **82–85**
Messianic banquet 55, 81, 132
Messianic Secret 18, 44, 51, 84–85
miracles 26–27, 77, 78–79, 115
mission 70–71, 120–121
Montefiore, Hugh 119
Moses 46, 80, 94, **141**
motivation 136–137
Mustard Seed, parable of 127

N

nature miracles 24, 26–27, 77
Neronian persecution 23
New Testament 8
non-violent protest 99

O

outcasts 104–109

P

Palestine 30
    religious and political groups 32–33
    unrest in 31
parables 76, **126–127**
paralysed man 88
Passion, The 16
Passion predictions 141
Passover 31, 50, 54
Paul 17, 19, 20, 71
Pentecostal churches 71
persecution 21, 23, 24
Person of Jesus 141
Peter
    call of 118
    calls Jesus the Christ 42
    denials 25, 122–123
    in Gethsemane 56, 57
    as role model 124
    source of information 14, 21
    and transfiguration 46, 47
Pharisees 23, 24, 35, 96, 100, **141**
Pilate, Pontius 30, 60–61
prejudice 109

R

rabbis 76
reasons for writing the Gospel 18–21
Resurrection 25, **68–73**
rich man and the Kingdom of God 130
role models 124–125
Rome 12
    early Church in 13, 22–23
    and Palestine 30–31
    taxation 100–101

S

Sabbath 94–97
Sadducees 32, 33
Sanhedrin 32, 52, 53, 58–59, 60, 98
Satan 40, **141**
science and miracles 115
scribes 32, 33, 88, 95, **141**
Second Coming 20
secular 102
secular authorities 102, 103
service 132–133, 137
sick, Jesus and the 110–115
Simon of Cyrene 15, 62
sinners, Jesus eating with 105
slavery 22
Son of David 141
Son of God 38, 46, 59, **90–91**
Son of Man 42, 44, 54, **86–89**
sources 14
    primary 14–15
    reliability of 17
    secondary 16–17
Sower, parable of 126

storm, calming of the 24, 26–27
Sunday as holy day 26, 72
symbolism
    at Jesus' baptism 38–39
    in feeding of the five thousand 80–81
    Jesus' final hours 65
    Jesus' temptation 40
    transfiguration 46–47
synagogues 35, 95, **141**

T

taxation, Roman 100–101, 104
teacher, Jesus as 76, 78–79, 126–127
Temple, the 34
    tearing of the curtain 65
    Temple Court 98–99
temptation of Jesus 40–41
tents 47
Teresa, Mother 135
tomb, the empty 68
transfiguration 46–47
treasury, the 141
Twelve, the 118
    calling of the first four 118–119
    the mission 120–121
    role models 124–125
    see also **disciples**; **Peter**

U

Ur Markus 16

V

violent protest 141

W

watershed 43
wealth, Jesus' teaching on 130
widow at the treasury 136–137
withered hand, man with 96
women 65, 68, 102

X

Zealots 33, 53, 100